S0-BEP-446

The Philosophical Series of the Higher Institute of Philosophy,
University of Louvain, Belgium

ONTOLOGY

by

Canon Fernand Van Steenberghen
Ph.D. (Agrégé), S.T.D.

Professor of Philosophy at the Higher Institute of Philosophy,
University of Louvain, Belgium

TRANSLATED BY

REV. MARTIN J. FLYNN, Ph.D. (Louvain), S.T.D.
Professor of Philosophy, Immaculate Conception Seminary,
Huntington, L.I., N.Y.

NEW YORK CITY

JOSEPH F. WAGNER, Inc.
London: B. Herder

Nihil Obstat:

JOHN M. FEARNS, S.T.D.
Censor Librorum

Imprimatur:

✠ FRANCIS CARDINAL SPELLMAN,
Archbishop of New York

NEW YORK, SEPTEMBER, 1952

TRANSLATOR'S PREFACE

To EXERCISE any degree of real influence on contemporary philosophical thought, the neo-scholastic movement must present Thomistic thinking in terms which, if not familiar, are readily understandable to the modern mind. The profound insights of Saint Thomas' metaphysical thought must, therefore, be reformulated in a way consonant with modern philosophical progress and the legitimate needs of our own period.

Canon Van Steenberghen's *Epistemology* attempted to do just that for the Thomistic theory of knowledge. This companion volume of *Ontology* is intended to give an equally critical and systematic exposition of the Common Doctor's science of being.

This aim and purpose explain several distinctive features of the present work which may cause some discussion among scholastics. Certain traditionally accepted opinions have received considerable revision. A number of topics usually found in scholastic treatises on ontology have been omitted, and others have received a much briefer treatment than would ordinarily be expected.

The author claims that his procedure is a faithful application of the spirit which animated Saint Thomas himself. The Angelic Doctor was characterized by his readiness to benefit by the labors of all the great philosophers in revising and developing his own views. Commentators have shown that the majestic simplicity of the *Summa Theologica* springs in large measure from the determination to clear away every encumbrance to the progress of thought.

Canon Van Steenberghen has cut through the notionalism, logicism, and rationalism which still persist in many fine textbooks, to reveal the profound existentialism inherent in the Thomistic theory of being. He develops that ontology not as a "metaphysics of essences or possibles," but as a genuine study of "to be." His treatment shows that the basic effort to explain existence must lead to the affirmation of the existence of God and an examination of God's attributes. This accounts for the inclusion here of matter usually developed in a distinct treatise on natural theology.

The present translation is based on the first French edition, incorporating a number of revisions suggested by the author in private conference and correspondence.

I wish to express my sincere appreciation to all those who have contributed to this translation. The Reverend James F. Coffey, Ph.D., D.D., the Reverend Martin J. Healy, D.D., the Reverend Francis X. Glimm, S.T.L., and the Reverend Francis M. Tyrrell, Ph.D., all of the Immaculate Conception Seminary, Huntington, Long Island, N. Y., have furnished valued comments and suggestions. My gratitude is also due to Miss Catherine Griffin and several others for typing successive revisions of the text; to Kevin Sullivan, M.A., Ph.L., for his care in editing the manuscript; and to Mr. Thomas J. Kennedy for assistance in preparing the index. I gladly express my debt to the Reverend David J. Lynch, S.T.D., of the Diocese of Brooklyn, N. Y., for many kindnesses which facilitated this undertaking.

I wish also to thank The Bruce Publishing Company for kind permission to use an illustration from C. N. Bittle's *The Science of Correct Thinking*.

MARTIN J. FLYNN.

AUTHOR'S INTRODUCTION

THIS treatise on ontology forms the sequel to our treatise on epistemology. The one purpose and the same critical point of view motivates both treatises. Our principal aim has been to show that the problems of metaphysics are in no sense arbitrary or artificial; their birth, specification, and final solution are determined by the demands of the reality present to consciousness and by the legitimate requirements of the mind itself. We have tried to develop the science of being in a strictly systematic way by eliminating all those foreign accretions which threaten to smother it in most classical text-books.

Like its predecessor, this work was written for students who are receiving their first introduction to philosophy. It was not written for specialists, and it does not claim in any way to be an exhaustive study of the problems of metaphysics.

Our treatment is often very abridged and concise. Consequently, it requires further development by the professor, and it leaves to him the task of completing the text of the treatise in his own way, depending on the time which he has at his disposal.

We have taken St. Thomas for our guide in both ontology and epistemology because his wonderful genius for clarity and balance in expression makes him the ideal master for young students. Furthermore, we believe that the deep insights which lie at the roots of his metaphysical thought are as valuable and productive as ever. It is only natural that we should owe a great deal to our colleague Professor Nicholas Balthasar, and to the lamented Canon Leon Becker, who died prematurely in 1925. It is to these two men of different temperaments and quite different methods that we owe our initiation into the secrets of metaphysics. However, while acknowledging the debt we owe to our former professors we do not wish to impute to them any responsibility for the views which will be defended in this book. These views are mainly the result of long personal reflection on the problems of ontology.

Our presentation of metaphysics in this treatise leads up to the affirmation of the Infinite Being as the creative, personal, and provident cause of the universe. In this sense the problem of God is, at one and the same time, the hidden dynamic behind the investigation and the culmination of the search which is so human and yet is so difficult for man. This remark merely serves to emphasize the pre-eminent place that metaphysical knowledge should have in an integral humanism, and the importance of a solid metaphysical training for that intellectual elite who will be called upon to reorientate our disorganized society. Furthermore, the conclusions of general metaphysics determine all further development in philosophy and play a most important part in theological speculation.

Louvain, Feb. 2, 1946.

TABLE OF CONTENTS

7

PART FOUR

INTRODUCTION TO ONTOLOGY

THE remarks which we will make in this section really lie outside the field of the science of being. Their only purpose is to furnish the reader with some useful data concerning the various names given to this science, the place that this investigation should hold in a systematic philosophy and, finally, the method used by the science.

§ 1. Names Given to the Science of Being

Aristotle can be called the creator of the science of being as being. He called it the *first philosophy*[1] because it considered the first principles and first causes. He thought that it enjoyed a primacy of excellence or dignity over all the other sciences. The name "first philosophy" can be kept in a sense, because the science of being is really first considering the excellence of its object and the place which it holds in a properly constructed system of philosophy. Together with epistemology, which serves as its introduction, it forms the basic philosophical discipline.[2] However, the expression "first philosophy" has this inconvenience that it does not tell us what the object of the science of being is.

Aristotle also called it the *divine science*[3] because it treats of the "most divine beings," that is, the substances which are separated from matter, and above them the Pure Act or the First Mover. As we understand the science of being today, it deserves the title of "divine science" even more than it did

---

1. πρώτη φιλοσοφία.
2. Fernand Van Steenberghen, *Epistemology*, trans. Martin J. Flynn (New York: Joseph F. Wagner, Inc., 1949), p. 295.
3. θεολογικὴ ἐπιστήμη.

for Aristotle, for the whole effort expended on it now leads
to the assertion of the existence of the Infinite Being as the
unique cause of everything distinct from Him, and the divine transcendence of this Infinite Being is incomparably
greater than the completely relative transcendence of the Pure
Act in Aristotle. Yet the name "divine science" is not entirely acceptable, because a science should be specified and
defined by its object, and God is not the object of the science
of being. God is the final term of this science because the
affirmation of the existence of God is the principal conclusion
which this science establishes.

Usually the science of being is called *metaphysics*. The
historical origin of this term was in no way related to the
object of the science which it came to designate. About the
year 50 B.C., Andronicus of Rhodes undertook to classify
the scholarly writings of Aristotle with a view to their
publication. Up to that time these writings had not been
circulated outside the relatively small group of pupils of
the Lyceum. In the classification worked out by Andronicus,
the different fragments which referred to the first philosophy
were grouped together into some fourteen books and were
placed after the books of natural philosophy or "physics."
For this reason, they were called τὰ (βιβλία) μετὰ τὰ φυσικά.
Later the expression was simply transposed into Latin, and
the fourteen books of the Stagirite became the *Metaphysica
Aristotelis,* or the *Libri Metaphysicae*. The scholastics of
the Middle Ages soon read a philosophical meaning into the
term *metaphysica:* they held that the science of being was so
called because it was "later than" and "superior to" physics
(post physicam et supra physicam). It was held to be later
because its object was reached by the third degree of abstraction, after one had gone beyond physical and mathematical abstraction. It was held to be superior because its

object, attained by the highest degree of abstraction, was considered to be entirely freed from matter. These points, however, are far from being certain. Furthermore, they entail grave inconveniences. First of all, the science of being does not in any way suppose a physics, whether we take "physics" to mean experimental physics or cosmology. It is completely independent of experimental physics; and cosmology, far from preceding general metaphysics, should be constructed as an extension of general metaphysics, which forms one of the branches of special metaphysics.[4] Again, it is not exact to picture the object of the science of being as if it were an intelligible completely freed from matter and situated "above" the physical or the sensible, somewhat after the fashion of the Platonic Ideas. We shall see that the science of being has as its object the concrete real taken in all its richness. If in spite of everything we still insist on giving a philosophical sense to the term "metaphysics," we should take it to mean the study of an object which is in some way "beyond" the physical, that is, beyond the phenomenon or sensible appearance. The science of being claims to study the thing in its most intimate reality, in all its concrete richness. In this sense "metaphysical" becomes a synonym for "metempirical."

In the seventeenth century, the term *ontology* began to be used to designate the science of being. The writings of Christian Wolff contributed to the wide use of this name in the following century. This is evidently the most simple and the most exact term. Some have rejected it, giving as a reason that the term "ontology" has been used sometimes in an idealistic sense to mean the science of the idea of being, or an a priori knowledge, without relation to experience. But most of the technical terms of philosophy have been

4. Van Steenberghen, *op. cit.*, pp. 288-89.

misused at one time or other, and the term "metaphysical" can cause just as much equivocation as the term "ontology." Thus, modern scholastics use the expression "metaphysical degrees" to signify aspects of one and the same substantial form which are only logically distinct.

This question of vocabulary is not, however, of first importance. Here we shall follow common usage and refer to the science of being, indifferently, as *ontology, general metaphysics,* or even simply, *metaphysics.*

§ 2. The Place which the Science of Being Holds in a System of Philosophy

A century-old controversy divides scholastics on the question of the proper classification of the philosophical disciplines. The first group, who can with some justification appeal to St. Thomas himself, accept the theory of the three degrees of abstraction, and they look upon ontology as the crown of speculative philosophy. For them, ontology is preceded not only by logic, but by cosmology, psychology, and mathematical philosophy. (This last, however, is ordinarily overlooked in spite of the importance given to the three degrees of abstraction.) The other group base their views on a different conception of the classification of the philosophical sciences. They consider ontology as the fundamental philosophical discipline, which is grafted immediately on epistemology; ontology or general metaphysics is, then, continued in a twofold special metaphysics, that of man and that of the material world.[5]

A complete discussion of this question would lead us far afield and would be out of place in this treatise. Here we

5. Some authors consider natural theology or theodicy a third branch of special metaphysics. This, however, is not the case since, as we shall see, the philosophical study of God is an integral part of ontology.

shall merely note that the second point of view seems to merit our unqualified acceptance. We have already stated this in our epistemology.[6] The other view shows too slavish an acceptance of the empiricism of Aristotle in trying to subordinate the study of metaphysical laws to a preliminary study of the material world. Furthermore, that view is strongly influenced by certain pedagogical considerations which are not justified, and it gives to the three degrees of abstraction a doctrinal importance that they do not actually have.[7]

The study which we are going to make here does not presuppose in our thought any other knowledge than that of epistemology (analytical, critical, and logical).

§ 3. *The Method Employed in the Science of Being*

It is impossible to determine, in an a priori way, the methods which will be used in the development of a science, but these methods will reveal themselves gradually as the search develops. We can, however, point out certain possibilities which present themselves even from the start, considering the nature of the object studied and the general conditions of progress in thought. Thus with respect to the science of being, the fact that we have discovered its object in analytical and critical epistemology, and have determined the laws of reasoning in logical epistemology, now permits us to fix in the following way the general method which imposes itself on an ontology from the very start.

The object of ontology is given or found in *any kind of experience whatever,* whether objective or subjective. This is because every human experience is necessarily an experi-

6. Van Steenberghen, *op. cit.,* pp. 284-91.
7. Van Steenberghen, "Réflexions sur la systématisation philosophique," *Revue Néoscolastique de Philosophie,* May, 1938, pp. 212-15.

ence of being. The intellect develops this experience by forming the *transcendental idea* of being. The *existential judgment* which restores the content of the concept of being to an object of experience, is an affirmation which has an absolute value. Ontology can use two methods in the further study of its object: first, it can turn to new experiences which reveal new modalities of being; secondly, it can use the deductive processes of reason to discover affirmations contained implicitly in the explicit affirmation of being, or in the affirmation of those modes of being which we know by experience. Only the actual development of metaphysics will allow us to state more precisely to what degree, and under what form, each of these two methods should be employed.

In an introduction of this sort it would be quite fitting to give a historical review stressing the main lines of the development of metaphysical problems in the course of time. This sort of review would help the reader to see better the importance of the questions which are to be treated. This was our intention in our epistemology where we gave an historical sketch of the evolution of the problem of knowledge from the beginnings of Greek philosophy.[8] But the metaphysical problem is much more complex than the epistemological problem, and unless our survey were to be left quite incomplete, we would have to devote a number of pages to it. For the time being it will be enough to ask the reader to consult some short sketch of the history of philosophy— paying particular attention to what concerns the history of metaphysics. A preparation of this sort will help him feel more at home with the study of ontology.[9]

8. Van Steenberghen, *Epistemology*, pp. 51-73.
9. See, for example, Louis De Raeymaeker, *Introduction to Philosophy*, trans. Harry McNeill (New York: Joseph F. Wagner, Inc., 1948), pp. 70-162.

Part One

BEING AND ITS ATTRIBUTES

Chapter I

BEING OR THE OBJECT OF ONTOLOGY

The object of ontology was given to us, in fact it forced itself upon us, in epistemology. The analysis of the elements making up my consciousness immediately presented me with being, or the real, as a first undeniable datum. Being is the object of my very first experience and of every other experience had later on. It is represented by my basic concept and is affirmed by my very first judgments. In epistemology we began our critique of knowledge with a critique of our knowledge of being. In that critique the absolute value of being itself and, consequently, of the judgment which expresses it, became clear to me. From that time we saw that it was possible to institute an inquiry which would try with the help of deductive reason to bring out the further affirmations contained implicitly in our first affirmation of the real, and in our affirmation of its basic modalities.

In other words, the starting point of ontology coincides perfectly with the starting point of epistemology. But while epistemology considers being from the point of view proper to that science, that is, as an element making up consciousness, ontology studies being considered in itself. Consequently, in order to determine as precisely as possible just what is the object of metaphysics, we have once more to resume, now from a new point of view and in a more profound way, the analysis and critique of our knowledge of being.

§ 1. The Material Object and the Formal Object of Ontology

My human knowledge begins on the level of experience: it begins (1) with objective experience which puts me in immediate contact with a world of corporeal objects, and (2) with subjective experience by which I become conscious of my own activity and of the active subject which is the principle of that activity. I am conscious that I seize being, or the real, in any experience whatever, no matter how fleeting, superficial, or ephemeral it may appear. An experience which was not an experience of being could only be an experience of non-being; this does not make sense. There can be no question, then, of having any privileged experience of being as such, since being as such reveals itself immediately and necessarily in every experience whatever. For my human consciousness, sense experience is an experience of being just as much as the intimate experience of the self. It is true that this last experience gives me modalities of being which are not had in objective experience, but these *particular* modalities are of little help when we try to grasp the basic value *common* to everything which is.

At the beginning of our inquiry the object of ontology is the same as the *complete object of my actual experience.* I propose to study everything which is given both in my subjective and objective experience, because everything which is given to me is given immediately and unquestionably as "something," as "real," as "being." Metaphysics, then, is a science which takes as its initial object any datum of experience whatever and, therefore, all the data of experience which are accessible or available to the metaphysician.

Regarding this first object let us note briefly that being is given to me first of all as a *fact*. I see that something exists, I do not know *why* something exists. I do not see any necessity in this fact, at least not immediately, except the need of affirming it. Secondly, the real which is given to me is evidently *complex;* that is, it involves a diversity of aspects, a multiplicity of modes, either simultaneous or successive, which we have already briefly described in epistemology.[1] As yet I am not stating anything about the nature of this complexity; I simply accept it as a first fact which is as undeniable as reality itself. Finally, I see that the real which is given to me is *not stable*. It implies a successive diversity, because the field of my experience is constantly changing.

The object of ontology which we just described is called the *material* object, that is, the "matter" which this science studies, in opposition to the *formal* object, that is, the "form," or "formality," or "point of view" from which the material object will be considered. The same material object can in fact be considered from very different points of view. What, then, is the formal object of ontology?

We know already that when a datum of experience is presented to the *conscious subject that I am,* I spontaneously react by conceiving the *idea* or *concept* of being. This means that I transfer the datum of experience to the level of perfect immanence in the form of a representation which is abstract, universal, and stable.[2] Now just as being or the real appeared to me to be the first object of my experience and the condition for every experience, so the concept of

1. Van Steenberghen, *Epistemology,* pp. 108-49.
2. *Ibid.,* pp. 130-31, 134.

being appears to me to be the fundamental concept from which I start to build up the entire structure of my intellectual representations. And since this concept of being represents impartially any object of experience whatever, it is clear that it can help to synthesize all my experiences. It has the function, then, of bringing out the *common value which is hidden in every object of experience.*

Metaphysics will undertake to study precisely this common value, to find out what it implies in the real, and what value this synthetic representation has. It will try to determine exactly what the unity is which is revealed and expressed by the concept of being. In other words, the formal object of metaphysics is the value of being which is included in every object of experience. Metaphysics studies the datum of experience in so far as it is *being,* and in so far as it is *real.*

This formal object determines or fixes the route we must follow, or the method of our investigation, from the very outset of our ontology. Since the formal object of this study is expressed in my thought by the idea of being, we must begin by investigating the exact meaning and value of this idea. The very possibility of making any further inquiry depends on the answer to this problem.

The concept of being shows itself most clearly in the affirmation of being, that is, in the *existential judgment* which I spontaneously make concerning any datum of experience whatever. By these judgments I restore to the datum the content of the idea which I had abstracted from it: "this *is;* that *exists;* that is *real."* Under different grammatical forms the predicates of these judgments indicate the fundamental value which I find in any object of experience whatever, and which I transfer to my intellectual consciousness under the form of an idea: the idea of being.

Let us look now at some of the distinctive properties of this idea of being.

§ 2. *The Comprehension of the Idea of Being*

1. *Being is Indefinable.*—What is the nature and comprehension of this idea?

When we wish to determine the nature of an object more precisely, we try to "define" it; that is, we try to situate it with respect to other objects, so that we can distinguish what is proper to it and mark off its limits. When, however, we try to define the predicate "to exist," or the content of the concept "being," we realize that this content is *indefinable*. To define a concept is, in fact, to oppose it to other concepts and to attach it to concepts which are more primitive, more simple, and more general. In brief, it means to *situate* it in a certain classification of concepts, which begins with the supreme "categories" or "general" and then descends through successive precisions down to the most specific concepts. But the only concept that opposes the concept of being is its own negation, or the concept of non-being. No concept can be more primitive, more simple, or more general than the concept of being because the concept of being is the *first* of all, and all other concepts imply it. The concept of being is the most *simple* because all other concepts are determinations, particularizations, and modes of it. It is the most *general* or the most *common* because, as we shall see immediately, only non-being lies outside its extension. The concept of being is therefore indefinable.

The fact that the idea of being cannot be defined merely expresses, on the conceptual plane, the impossibility of defining being or the real itself, the first object of our experience. For it is the very nature of being, as given to us, not to have any determined essence, but rather to go beyond and to include all determined essences, that is, all the "modes" of being. Being is therefore truly the *primum notum;* it is strictly *per se notum,* for nothing is clearer, or more simple, or more evident for the intellect than being itself. Far from being known or explained by anything other than itself, it is the principle of knowledge. It is the object of our very first experience, and it is also the source of our very first concept. It has been correctly stated that man is an animal who understands the word "is." The proposition "this exists," has an immediate meaning for man.[3]

Being is the first evidence; it is the source of all other evidence. It cannot receive any genuine explanation, because everything which would be used to explain being would be more complex than being and would presuppose it. By continued reflection we must try to bring home to ourselves the extraordinary and unique power which is implied in our capacity to know the real or being, or in our capacity to say "that *is.*" Matter exists, but it does not know that it exists. I know that it exists, and I know that I exist. I do not understand *why* a thing exists, but I do understand *that* something exists. In other words I am "intelligent," that is, "capable of knowing being."

Here we can see the basic error committed by every so-called "metaphysics of essences or possibles," that is, by every metaphysics which tries to leave aside the existence or actuality of things and to limit itself to the study of the "essential laws" or the "necessary possibility" of reality. Under the pretense that we do not know *why* something exists, or that we do not know *fully* the mystery of existence, or that we cannot know being in the way in which we know essences —that is, by defining them and classifying them in genera

3. *Ibid.,* pp. 82-83.

and species—these views actually lose sight of the fundamental intelligible which is the formal object of the intelligence, and the only intelligible which is intelligible of itself.

2. *Improper Definitions.*—There are certain procedures
which we might try to utilize in attempting to define the
content of the concept of being, or the "essence of being."
But these procedures are only of psychological interest.
They can help to arouse our attention or to shake off routine,
and they may suggest novel aspects of the way in which the
intellect grasps being.

Thus we can try to define being by opposing it to non-
being. We have said that to define is to try to situate. But
when we try to situate the idea of being, we see that the
attempt is absolutely fruitless, for being is opposed only to
its own negation, non-being, which evidently has no solidity.
By defining being as "that which is not nothing" we bring
out the supreme simplicity of the idea of being. This, however, is a definition only in a very improper sense. It is a
mere artifice of thought. To see anything more in the statement would be to fall into a vicious circle, since the idea of
non-being presupposes the idea of being, and therefore cannot throw any real light upon it.

To define the idea of being we spontaneously turn to
*experiences and ideas which seem to be more familiar or
more expressive.* We are baffled by the simplicity of this
idea and by the mystery which envelops it. But once again
we must avoid a snare.

Philosophers of an empiricist bent, who try to reduce
everything to the solidity of brute fact, will readily define
being as the basic "supposite." They prefer to find being in
perceived objects—not in the changeable aspects of these

objects, but rather in those aspects which seem to be fixed and permanent. They hold that it is the *"substance* of the things of experience" which is being in a pre-eminent sense. Their contention has some force, for being of itself implies duration or permanence. Nevertheless, being is simpler and broader than "subject" or "substance"; for everything that can affect a subject, all the changes that can happen to a substance, and every activity of which it can be the source, are also being or reality.

On the other hand, philosophers with an idealist turn of mind, who are obsessed by the absolute autonomy of thought, cannot resign themselves to accepting being as a mere fact. They claim to find the "how," the "why," and the "essence" of being in "thought in act." They define the idea of being in terms of "act" or "activity." Believing that they discover in our consciousness of spiritual activities a certain way of "producing" or of "placing" being, they believe that they have discovered its secret; they hold that to grasp the essence of being means to seize ourselves in the "exercise of existence as the final act." Such psychological analyses are interesting and useful, provided that we do not mistake their true meaning. "Being" always implies "actuality," but "being" is simpler and broader than "act." It is simpler because "act" and "activity" are already "modes of being." It is broader because "act" is opposed to "potency," and "activity" is opposed to "subject." [4] Being, however, is not opposed to anything; it designates the potency and the subject as well as the act and activity. Consequently, to define being as the "exercise of the last act," is evidently not exact (because everything is "being," and not merely the last act). It is to define what is more clear by what is more

4. *Ibid.,* pp. 104-05.

obscure, for "exercise," "act," and "last," are more obscure notions than "being." [5]

It is sometimes said that being is the "supreme value" or the "value in se," in opposition to the "phenomena," or those aspects which appear to me, or which merely have "value for me." Such definitions are also inadequate, for the "non-supreme" values are still being, and the "phenomenon" could not have "value for me" unless it had a "value in se" or the value of being. Non-being cannot "appear" to me or form a "value for me." Furthermore, it is quite evident that the notion of "value" is not clearer than the notion of being.

3. *Consequences for Terminology.*—These spontaneous attempts to define being by more complex notions also carry over into an author's choice of terminology. The idea of being can be expressed by different grammatical forms: by verbs, nouns (substantives and adjectives), and by participles.

Verb forms: "this *is,* this *exists.*"

To say "me *to exist*" (that is, "to exist" belongs to me) may be grammatically bad English, but it is metaphysically accurate.

Noun forms: "this is *something,* a *thing,* an *entity,* an *essence,* a *reality,* a *being,* this is *real.*"

Participial forms: "this is *existing,* this is *being.*"

The verb forms are derived from the ideas of *act* or *activity;* being is represented as the exercise of an *act* or of an *activity.* The noun forms recall the idea of *"subject"* or of

5. When St. Thomas speaks of the *esse* which is the *ultimate act,* he is referring to the *esse* which is the principle or ontological component of finite being. He is not speaking of the *being* which is the "first known," the formal object of metaphysics.

"thing." Being is presented as the fundamental *subject.* Finally, the participle is a combination of the noun and the verb; "existing" signifies "the subject which exists." But since all these notions are inadequate with respect to the notion of being, the terms listed should be taken as *synonyms.* There is only a purely grammatical difference between them. The expressions, "Socrates *exists"* and "Socrates is *real,"* "Socrates is *something,"* "Socrates is *existent,"* are all equivalent.

Consequently, we cannot say that the conceptual duality "essence" and "existence," or the "essence-existence" relation, is primitive and irreducible. This duality is not implied in any way in the idea of being. If in our simplest judgment ("Something exists") we naturally distinguish between the subject which exists and the act of existing, this is because we always grasp being in a particular experience (that is, as "something," as "this"), and we directly oppose the idea of being ("exists") to the particular mode that we see; but this idea of being could be equally well expressed by a noun by saying, "This is *real,"* or "This is a *reality."* [6]

In brief, then, my notion of being expresses any experience whatsoever without any particular determination or limit which would help me to define its content. To conceive being is to become aware, on the occasion of any experience whatever, that something *exists* without knowing *why* this something exists.

6. M. D. Roland-Gosselin, *Essai d'une étude critique de la connaisance* (Paris, 1932), pp. 62-67. The author seems at first to consider the duality of "essence-existence" as primitive, but toward the end of the work he recognizes the derived and secondary character of "essence."

an aspect, element, or determination which could be separated even in a logical sense from other aspects, for all the other determinations are still intrinsically and formally being.

§ 4. The Extension of the Idea of Being

1. *Transcendental Extension.*—The extension of a concept refers to the degree of universality which it has. A further reflection on the comprehension of the idea or concept of being will show us that the extension of this concept also has a unique character.

If the concept of being represents a note which is really common to everything which is not non-being, and if the content of this concept can be defined only by opposition to non-being, then it becomes clear at once that the only condition required for the concept of being to represent anything is that this thing should not be pure non-being. On the other hand, the fact that my experience is being continually broadened by new data appearing in my consciousness would suggest that perhaps my past and present experiences are not equivalent to all possible experience, and particularly are not equivalent to all reality. It suggests that reality as known by me might not be tantamount to the real as such. Whatever may be said about this point, the knowledge which I have of the real given in my experience suffices to show me that if there exists anything outside my experience, then this "outside" can be and is adequately represented by my concept of being. Otherwise it would have to be identified with non-being pure and simple.

Thus we see another essential characteristic of the concept of being, that is, its *transcendental* extension. In traditional terminology, "transcendental" refers to a notion whose extension or universality surpasses or "transcends" that of all other notions *(transcendit species et genera)*. Its extension is unlimited. A notion of this sort synthesizes all the real. Now the concept of being fulfills this requirement because it can be predicated of everything which is not pure non-being. Consequently, this concept of being is transcendental.

The concept of being constitutes a confused but adequate representation of the whole universe, including everything which could exist outside my experience. To know a datum as being means to recognize, at least implicitly, that this datum is related to all reality without any exception.

Because the concept of being gives man's thought this transcendental perspective, it destroys the basic principles of Kantian empiricism. It is simply not true to say that every legitimate operation of the understanding must stop at the borders of our experience or at the limits of the world of phenomena. I can grasp being in any experience, and by that very fact I can know in a confused but actual way the sum total of reality.

Some authors have tried to represent the Principle of Immanence as the irrefutable axiom of idealism, but in reality it provides a perfect formula for the most emphatic type of metaphysical realism. The statement, "Anything outside thought is unthinkable," is true in the sense that the object of thought is being and anything outside being is impossible.

The concept of being, then, helps me to develop my own limited experience and infinitely to surpass it. Because of that concept I can pass from the singular judgment, "This exists," to the absolutely universal principle, "Anything exists," in which the subject "anything" designates equally well every object given in my experience and everything which lies outside my experience.[15]

15. Van Steenberghen, *op. cit.*, pp. 186-88.

2. *The Existence of an Absolute Reality.*—The transcendental extension of the concept of being will reveal to us the existence of an *absolute or unconditioned reality,* and will make it possible for us to build our ontology upon an absolutely unshakable foundation.

Being is given to us a fact: I see that something exists; I see that I exist. But my curiosity does not cease with the acquisition of that fact; it demands further satisfaction. I want to know how and why something exists. I would like to know the thing's "reason for existence." I exist. That is an undeniable fact which forces every intelligence to affirm that I exist. I exist at a certain point in the flow of time. It will, therefore, be eternally necessary to affirm and to recognize that I existed at that moment. But is my existence necessary in itself? Does it impose itself? It does give rise to a certain necessity of the logical order (that is, the need of affirming it—a necessity which is common to all true judgments), but does it imply any necessity of the ontological or real order? Does it imply a necessity of existing? This is by no means evident. If I were only being, if I had only the quality "existence," I would be opposed only to non-being, and since I would be opposed to nothing, I could not depend on anything, I would be my own reason for existence and no problem would arise regarding my existence. But reality is much more complex than that. I am "being," but I am also "such"; I am a "self," and I am opposed to the "non-self"; I am a "finite being" among numerous other finite beings. Now I believe that I see in the world of my experience (whether rightly or wrongly makes little difference at this time) certain finite beings which are "relative" to others; they are "conditioned" or "caused" by others. This animal owes his existence to another animal; the form of this liquid is determined by the shape of this bottle; I de-

pend on the air which I breathe, on the foods which nourish
me. The concepts of "relative" and "absolute" are thus
formed in my mind. I call a thing which depends in any way
on another thing "relative" or "conditioned." I call a thing
which does not depend on anything else "absolute" or "unconditioned." [16]

Armed with these notions let us now turn to the object of
ontology. By the aid of the transcendental concept, which is
the confused representation of the real considered as a whole
without any other restriction or limitation than non-being, I
can now see the sort of existence which belongs to the real
taken as a whole. I can see at once that whereas the hypothesis of relativity can and should be raised for particular
realities, it cannot be raised regarding the sum total of
reality, that is, for "everything which exists." This is so because the "whole" as such cannot depend on anything else
and, therefore, it must suffice for itself. Indeed that which
is not opposed to anything cannot be relative or dependent.
That which is opposed only to non-being can depend only on
non-being, and to depend on non-being is really not to depend at all. Now the sum-total of reality is opposed only to
non-being; therefore, the totality of reality cannot be relative, but must be absolute or unconditioned.

We must be very careful in stating the exact meaning of
this important conclusion. For the sum-total of reality to be
absolute as a totality, it would be sufficient for one element
at least of this totality to be absolute, and for the others to
depend on that first element. The proposition, "Everything is
relative or conditioned," is evidently false. To contradict it,
it is enough to state that "something is absolute or unconditioned " Let us guard, however, against making any hasty
statements about the nature of the "total reality," and conse-

16. *Ab-solutum:* freed from, independent of.

quently about the nature of the "absolute reality" which it unquestionably involves. Is the "whole" one unique being, or is it a plurality of beings? And in the second hypothesis, are all these beings unconditioned, or are some of them conditioned by others? These questions have still to be answered. We have, however, shown that an absolute reality exists.

Consequently, not every existent thing can be dependent or relative. Something exists of itself and by itself; something imposes itself; something is necessary of itself; something must be and cannot *not* be. The real implies an absolute and unconditioned value. It finds its reason for existence in itself; it contains its own *why* or *explanation*. In critical epistemology we saw that every true judgment had a characteristic necessity. Now we see that necessity appearing in the object of the judgment as a necessity of existence.

Let us note, however, that this ontological necessity shows itself to us in a fact, and as a fact. *Since* something exists, then something exists by itself, for the proposition, "Everything exists by something else," is evidently contradictory; that is, it destroys itself. We know *that* an absolute reality exists, but we do not know *why* it exists.[17]

§ 5. Conclusions

This examination of the object of metaphysics now allows us to draw some important conclusions concerning the nature of the science of being.

The *material object* of this science, which was limited at first to my field of experience, has now been enlarged in the light of the formal object until it embraces all reality whatsoever. Its material object therefore is unlimited. But all

17. Van Steenberghen, *op. cit.,* pp. 187-88.

the other sciences have a limited object. None of them claims to study an object transcending the world of human experience or the phenomenal world.

The *formal object* of this science coincides with its material object, since the concept of being which is its expression is the adequate representation of the concrete reality. All the other sciences take some partial aspect of the material object for their formal object. And let us note further that the formal object of ontology coincides with the formal object of the intellect, or with the fundamental intelligible.

The *laws* and *principles* of metaphysics are a conceptual but adequate expression of the conditions of the concrete reality and of the nature of the concrete real. Metaphysical laws are developed as implications of the absolutely necessary affirmation of being. Consequently, these metaphysical laws will also be absolutely necessary.[18] The laws which the other sciences formulate regarding their abstract formal object represent real conditions only in an inadequate, partial, and schematic way. And since their formal object is some datum of experience which does not impose itself with absolute necessity, these scientific laws will express merely a factual order possessing no absolute necessity.

Ontology is the only science which studies existence as such. Beginning with the affirmation of the existent thing, it tries to determine how and why things exist. It studies *that which is,* precisely *in so far as it is—ens in quantum ens, ens in quantun est.* Metaphysics, as we have just defined it, is a science which pre-eminently merits the name *"existential."*

This interpretation of the object of metaphysics runs counter to the view held generally by modern scholasticism.

18. These characteristics will stand out more clearly on further examination of the metaphysical laws.

Opposition to empiricism and the influence of rationalism have caused modern scholastics to try to free the object of metaphysics from every bond with actual experience. They want the object of metaphysics to include the future, the past, and the possible. These are not included in actual experience because they do not actually exist.

For this reason scholastics distinguish between *ens formaliter sumptum* and *ens materialiter sumptum*. They say that in its formal sense being signifies the subject which exists, considered in so far as it exists, or considered in so far as it actually participates in the act of existing *(ens ut participium)*, or considered in so far as it "exercises" its act of existing *(ens in actu exercito)*. On the other hand, they say that being taken in its material sense signifies the subject considered independently of actual existence or the actual exercise of its act. It signifies every subject which has *any sort of relation* to existence (whether that relation be present, past, future, or possible). It is being as expressed by a noun *(ens ut nomen)*, since the noun in grammar designates an object independently of the acts which it exercises. Or, finally, it is the subject whose act is "designated," without affirming that it really exercises that act at this time *(ens in actu signato)*.

Having defined these notions, these authors then state that the object of metaphysics is not *ens formaliter sumptum* but *ens materialiter sumptum*. They hold that metaphysics studies "everything which is or can be," or more simply "everything which can be"; that is, the object of metaphysics must abstract from actual existence because while "to be" states merely a contingent fact, "to be able to be" states a necessity.

As a consequence, metaphysics becomes the science of the

"possibles" or "essences" which have a relation to existence, but it ceases to be the science of the existent thing.

We cannot accept the above definition of the object of ontology because this view seems to introduce complications which are useless and unnecessary. Useless, because we can surpass empiricism without resort to this round-about way. We can do so by bringing out in strong relief the transcendental character of the concept of being and the ontological necessity manifested by reality as a whole. Unnecessary, because we know the possible and possibility only in the existent thing and through the existent thing. *Ab esse ad posse valet illatio.* Consequently, to introduce the notion of the possible at this point is entirely superfluous. Finally, we lose nothing by excluding the past, the future, and the possible as such from the object of metaphysics, since as such they do not exist. The past was the object of metaphysics; the future will be the object at some future time; the possible could have been the object of metaphysics. The past, the future, and the possible are included in the object of metaphysics in the measure in which they are precontained in their causes, and to the extent to which these causes actually exist.

Furthermore, the position of these modern scholastics labors under serious disadvantages. It introduces a confusing terminology by holding that being taken materially is the *formal* object of the science of being. But—what is far more serious—it separates in the thing the *subject* which is and the *act of existing,* because it considers being in abstraction from its actual existence. In the real order such a separation is meaningless. A thing which does not exist, is nothing; a thing which does not have the act of existing, is not even a "subject." In brief, we cannot "disexistentiate" a being without completely destroying it; *quod potest esse sed non est, potest esse aliquid, sed non est aliquid.* Furthermore, as we said above, at the start of metaphysics there is no place for a distinction in reality between subject and act, between essence and existence. Such a distinction would be only grammatical.[19] *Ens materialiter sumptum* is therefore unthinkable and impossible.[20] To say that the object of metaphysics abstracts from actual existence, really means that its object is reduced to the ideal or conceptual order, for concepts are the only things which abstract from the actual existence of the objects which they represent.

19. See above, § 2, n. 3.
20. We can distinguish between *participium* and *nomen* when speaking about the *activity* of a subject. For example, the act of studying properly specifies the student *as* student, but he still remains a substantial being even when he stops studying. However, if a student ceases to exist, he also ceases to be a substantial being.

CHAPTER II

THE ATTRIBUTES OF BEING AND THE FIRST PRINCIPLES

UP TO this point our metaphysical reflection has swung between two poles: between reality as given in any experience whatever and the concept of being which is the adequate representation of that real in the immanence of consciousness. Can we make any further progress in our knowledge of being as such? Does reality as such have any distinctive "attributes" which we have not yet emphasized? Might there be certain "properties" common to everything which exists? Can we express them in concepts? How can we discover them and how define them?

Philosophers have always been interested in this problem of the basic attributes of the real. Greek antiquity tried to probe more deeply into the notions of unity, truth, and goodness. The Middle Ages revived these themes and developed them. At the beginning of the thirteenth century, Phillip the Chancellor wrote the first treatise on the transcendental properties. St. Thomas distinguished six transcendentals: *ens, res, aliquid, unum, verum, bonum.* The problem is much to the fore in our own times, notably in the question of the philosophy of values, since the transcendental properties are very properly considered the "supreme values."

We will try to make a rigorous derivation of these attributes in the pages which follow.

§ 1. *The Derivation of the Attributes of Being*

What is meant by the attributes of every being?

We cannot expect new experiences to give us distinct entities which would serve as properties of every being as being. When I have once grasped the transcendental value of being in any experience, new experiences can only furnish me with modalities of being, or with further particular determinations of being.

A being in so far as it exists cannot be affected by a particular determination, because whatever affects a being in so far as it exists must affect equally well every other being, in so far as it is. It must, therefore, constitute a common or transcendental determination, not a particular determination. Experience, consequently, cannot give me the attributes of being as such.

To develop our knowledge of being as such, we must use the mind's discursive activity and try in this way to discover in the real as such *new intelligible aspects* which can be expressed by *new concepts.* The intelligence is the faculty of being; it is also the faculty of the relations affecting the real. It is a faculty of comparison. It seizes the oppositions and agreements existing in the real. Thus the problem of the attributes of every being reduces itself to the following: what are the basic relations which affect every being in so far as it exists?

A relation can be one of *opposition,* or one of *agreement;* it can be a relation which is *extrinsic* or *intrinsic* to the being under consideration. Let us examine these different possibilities with respect to any being considered in so far as it exists.

Every being in so far as it exists is opposed absolutely to non-being, and only to non-being. This constitutes an extrinsic relation of opposition which gives rise to a first attribute; every being is *distinct or determined in so far as it is.*

Considered in itself, every being in so far as it exists is opposed to the many different finite modes in which it appears. This is an intrinsic relation of opposition which discloses a second attribute: *indivision or the internal unity of everything which is.*

On the other hand, every being in so far as it exists is similar to every other being in so far as that exists. This is an extrinsic relation of agreement which is expressed in a third attribute: *ontological similarity.*

There is also a relation of agreement between every being and the spiritual consciousness, which is defined as a capacity for being or a transcendental capacity. This relation implies two final attributes: every being is *intelligible or true;* every being is *desirable or good,* in so far as it exists.[1]

This derivation of attributes can be represented by the following schema:

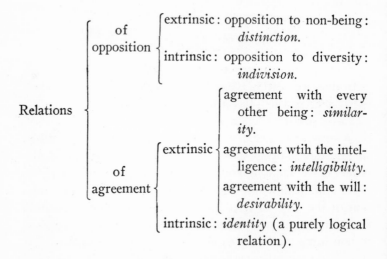

Relations
- of opposition
  - extrinsic: opposition to non-being: *distinction.*
  - intrinsic: opposition to diversity: *indivision.*
- of agreement
  - extrinsic
    - agreement with every other being: *similarity.*
    - agreement wtih the intelligence: *intelligibility.*
    - agreement with the will: *desirability.*
  - intrinsic: *identity* (a purely logical relation).

1. Only one other intrinsic relation of agreement may be found in every being, namely, the identity of being with itself. This relation, however, is a purely logical construct resulting from mental duplication. Consequently, no new ontological attribute may be derived from it.

The transcendental attributes give rise to the first principles of metaphysics. A judgment which is universal and fundamental is termed a "principle," because judgments of this sort are found at the starting point or "principle" of many processes of deduction. These first principles govern all our intellectual life; they express the most basic laws and relations of reality. Our study of the object of metaphysics has served to bring out the two basic metaphysical affirmations: "Something exists," and "Something exists of itself." However, these judgments are not principles because they are not universal judgments.[2] The first metaphysical principles will result from the attribution of the transcendental properties to being.

We must now examine each of these properties more closely.

§ 2. Distinction

Every being in so far as it exists is distinct or determined.

In this proposition the subject refers to any object whatever which can be represented by the concept of being. As we have already seen, a being in so far as it is, is opposed only to non-being, that is, to the negation of being. When we consider a being in so far as it exists, and try to discover in it some relation of opposition to an extrinsic object, we see at once that we can conceive only one relation of the sort, namely, the relation of absolute opposition to non-being. Every being in so far as it exists is opposed to non-being, and only to non-being. This amounts to say-

2. This first affirmation could give rise to the principle: "Every object which is given in my experience, or which is situated beyond my experience, exists." This is tantamount to saying that being or existence is a transcendental attribute. The completely general statement, "Everything which exists, exists," is an obvious tautology.

ing that it is not opposed to anything, or that it does not oppose anything, since non-being is only a being of reason which has no ontological reality. In other words, a being in so far as it exists excludes all relativity, dependence, determinability, and confusion with any other thing. It is in the highest degree distinct or determined. To exist is to be distinct or determined.

The very simple reasoning process which we have just developed, involves the following steps: (a) the affirmation of *being;* (b) the search for a *relation of opposition* between being and something extrinsic to it; (c) formation of the concept of *non-being;* (d) affirmation of the absolute *distinction* or supreme determination of being.

This first attribute of being is expressed in the metaphysical principle of distinction: *Every being in so far as it exists is distinct or determined.* This principle is very simple and has apparently no great significance; but in reality it has astonishing implications, as the further development of ontology will prove. Even at the present time, however, we can indicate some of its important consequences by showing that the principle of distinction is the ultimate foundation for the laws of thought, or the laws of logic. The reason for this is that it lies at the root of the first principles of logic, the principles of identity, non-contradiction, and the excluded middle.[3]

Let us examine briefly the nature and ultimate foundation of these principles of the logical order.

1. *The Principle of Identity.*—We do not here intend to speak about the principle which some authors call the *meta-*

---

3. Contrary to what many authors hold, these three principles are really logical laws, or laws of thought as such. They are not laws of the real order. See on this point A. Mansion, "Sur la correspondance du logique et du réel, *"Revue Néoscolastique de Philosophie,* August, 1932, pp. 311-18.

physical principle of identity, and which they formulate in the following way: "Being is being," or "That which is, is that which is." These formulae are mere tautologies, and in our opinion they are completely sterile, since they are not really judgments at all. We can justify the existence of two terms (subject and predicate) in a judgment only if the predicate is not exactly the same as the subject, but rather testifies to a certain progress in our knowledge of the subject expressed.[4] Now a purely tautological statement excludes any distinction between the subject and predicate. Consequently, a tautological statement cannot be a genuine judgment. Taken by itself the explicit formula of the tautological statement does not express anything.[5]

We are speaking now of the logical law of identity considered as the first basic law governing our processes of thought. Here again the principle of identity is often presented in a tautological fashion: "A is A." But if we consider the merits of this formula in itself, the formula does not seem to make much sense—for the reason given above. After all, what is the fundamental law governing all the activity of the human mind and all the logical order? It is the law which expresses the nature of affirmation or the affirmative judgment, because the act of judging is the principal act of our intelligence. The judgment in fact completes the elementary act of knowledge, and the judgment is the basis for all further reasoning activity.[6] We can state this law as follows: "In every correct affirmation, the predicate can be identified with the subject." In other words, every

4. Van Steenberghen, *Epistemology,* p. 144.
5. As a matter of fact, those who defend the "metaphysical principle of identity" seem to be alluding to the *identity* of being with itself. They would express themselves more accurately by saying: "Every being is identical to itself." Regarding this principle, see above, § 1, footnote 1.
6. Van Steenberghen, *op. cit.,* p. 145.

correct affirmation should be of this type: "S is P." This last formula gives us the universal form of the judgment or affirmation. The judgment attributes a predicate to a subject which really possesses it. It implies the basic identity of the two terms. It unifies what the mind had divided by abstraction.

What is the final basis for this logical law? In the last analysis, what is it that gives meaning to the affirmation as such? What is it that gives firmness, stability, and necessity to every true judgment? It is the absolute distinction of that which is, from that which is not. Or, it is the perfectly determined character of that which is, in so far as it is. If this distinction were not had, then no judgment would be consistent; there would be no such thing as stable truth, and no such thing as legitimate logical identity.

2. *The Principle of Non-Contradiction.*—Aristotle and St. Thomas did not recognize the principle of identity. For them, the first principle was the principle of non-contradiction: *We cannot affirm and deny the same predicate of the same subject;* or more briefly, *We cannot contradict ourselves.* Contradiction introduces discord into thought, ruins knowledge, and destroys itself.

Why? What is the ultimate foundation of this logical law? Once again, it is the basic distinction between that which is and that which is not. Now contradiction would deny this absolute distinction, since it tends to identify being and non-being. Consequently, it is not at all surprising that it leads to the destruction, that is to say, to the "annihilation" of knowledge.

3. *The Principle of the Excluded Middle.*—This third law of thought can be stated as follows: *There is no middle*

course between affirmation and negation. In other words, when we form a judgment about an object, affirmation and negation are the only possible alternatives. Any third hypothesis is inconceivable. Another form of the same principle states: *It is impossible to have a judgment which would be neither true nor false.*

Here again the ultimate metaphysical basis for this law is the absolute distinction between that which is and that which is not. A being in so far as it exists is opposed only to non-being. There is no conceivable intermediary between being and non-being, between to exist and not to exist. To be or not to be are the only possible alternatives.

The reader will have noted that we have been speaking about the *ultimate foundation* for these logical laws. We should note carefully that the elementary act of knowledge which forms the starting point for all our judging activity provides the proximate foundation and a sufficient critical explanation for these logical laws. We recognize that every logical process which respects this initial elementary act of knowledge, and limits itself to developing that knowledge, should be accepted as legitimate or correct.[7]

§ 3. Indivision: Unity

Every being is one or undivided in so far as it exists.

Distinction or opposition to non-being is the only relation of opposition *extrinsic* to a being which affects every being as being. We may now inquire whether any relation of opposition can be found within every being as being.

We are conscious already that reality as given in our experience presents a multiplicity of aspects or modes opposing one another and excluding one another. Further-

7. *Ibid.,* pp. 237-41.

more, in the world of our experience we perceive complex "things," that is, objects which possess a certain unity, yet which reveal a multiplicity of elements or "parts." Our own "self" manifests this double aspect. Consequently, it is only natural that we should ask what relation is had between being and the multiple or the diverse, between being and its many modes.

Can a being be multiple or "several," or differentiated, in so far as it exists? In other words, can we identify being as such with multiplicity as such? It is enough to raise these questions to see that there is an intrinsic relation of opposition between any being in so far as it is and the multiple modes which can affect it in itself. For the only opposition that a being implies, in so far as it exists, is opposition to non-being. Multiplicity, on the other hand, implies an opposition of elements, a diversity, an internal division. Consequently, a being cannot be multiple or divided in so far as it exists.

We see, then, that a being considered as being cannot explain the multiplicity, or internal opposition, which may actually affect it. Every being in so far as it exists is one or undivided. Just as it excludes all extrinsic opposition, so it also excludes all intrinsic division. There is antagonism between being as such and multiplicity as such. Being is not multiple or diverse of itself.

We can sum up as follows this reasoning process which enables us to set forth the second attribute common to every being: (a) the affirmation of *being;* (b) the search for a *relation of opposition* between being and something *intrinsic* to it; (c) the affirmation of the *multiple* or the *diverse;* (d) the discovery of the *unity* or *indivision* of every being in so far as it exists.

A very simple reasoning process is here involved:

Major: To be is not to oppose oneself to anything.
Minor: To be multiple is to oppose oneself to something.
Conclusion: To be is not to be multiple.

A new metaphysical principle is thus established: *Every being is one or undivided in so far as it exists.* This is a very simple principle, but its rich implications will become evident as our inquiry develops.

§ 4. Similarity

Every being is similar to every other being in so far as it exists.

We have seen all the relations of opposition which can affect every being in so far as it is being. We have now to determine what relations of agreement may be common to everything existing. We shall consider first the possible extrinsic relations of agreement.

When we re-examine our experience of multiplicity and diversity, it is obvious that there is some multiplicity in reality, whatever the exact nature of this multiplicity may be. Surely this tree is not the same as that other tree, nor is it the same as the animal which grazes close by. I myself am opposed to everything surrounding me. And yet in so far as I exist, I am opposed only to non-being. It is in so far as I am "such" a being that I am opposed to other beings which are "such" beings. Far from opposing others in so far as I exist, I am really in communion with them; I bear a resemblance to them by my entire being. Between them and myself there is a basic kinship. In brief, every being in so far as it exists gives rise to a relation of metaphysical similarity to every other being. This relation constitutes a third attribute common to everything which exists.

We can sum up the steps involved in the derivation of this new attribute as follows: (a) the affirmation of *being;* (b) the search for a *relation of agreement* between any being whatever and that which is *extrinsic* to it; (c) the affirmation of the *multiple* or of other beings; (d) the discovery of ontological *similarity.*

This furnishes us with a new metaphysical principle: *Every being is similar to every other being in so far as it exists.* We shall make use of it later.

§ 5. Intelligibility

Every being is intelligible or true in so far as it exists.

We may now ask whether besides similarity there are any other extrinsic relations of agreement found in a being considered in so far as it exists. The critique which we made of our knowledge of being in epistemology showed us that our intellectual consciousness had a transcendental capacity. Our study of the extension of the concept of being emphasized this remarkable characteristic of our thought still further.[8] Due to this concept of being, I possess a confused but adequate knowledge of everything which exists. On the other hand, it follows that everything which exists can be assimilated by my thought, at least in so far as it exists. Consequently, there is a relation of agreement between every being in so far as it exists and my intellect. Every being is intelligible in so far as it exists.

This process of reasoning can be summed up in the following way: (a) the affirmation of *being;* (b) the search for a new *relation of agreement* between a being and something *extrinsic* to it; (c) the affirmation that the *intellect* is

8. *Ibid.,* pp. 186-88. See also above, chap. I, 64, n. 1.

the faculty of being; (d) the discovery of the relation of *intelligibility*.

Every being is intelligible in so far as it exists. Like all the preceding principles, this principle will reveal important consequences later.

In traditional terminology, the intelligibility of being was called "ontological truth." Ontological truth was therefore defined as the property, possessed by every being in so far as it existed, of being assimilable or knowable by the intellect. This ontological truth, or truth of being, provided the foundation for *logical truth,* or truth of thought, that is, the conformity of the intellect (or more precisely of the judgment) to the being which is known. This latest attribute of every being requires further explanation.

The statement that every being is intelligible in so far as it exists does not imply in any way that my intellect actually has a distinct and explicit knowledge of everything which exists. (My intellect is the only one which I know at this time.) Nor am I claiming that every existing thing could be known in distinct fashion by my intellect. Rather I know that my explicit knowledge is limited to the field of my subjective and objective experience. I have no reason to suppose that nothing exists outside my actual or possible experience. Consequently, the metaphysical principle of intelligibility does not exclude a certain amount of genuine agnosticism.[9]

On the other hand, the intelligibility of every being as being implies that everything which exists can be seized by

9. This agnosticism is implicit in the empiricism of Aristotle which was adopted in large part by St. Thomas. For Aristotle, only what was *given* in or *implied* by experience was knowable; thus, starting from the movements of the stars he concluded that a certain number of spiritual substances do exist. As a philosopher, St. Thomas considers the existence of such spiritual substances (angels) as little more than a hypothesis suggested by the universal order. In this, then, he is even more agnostic than Aristotle.

my intellect in a confused way at least, and that in a certain sense nothing can escape my intellect since nothing escapes its formal object. In this connection we can give a somewhat new sense to the celebrated formula, *Anima est quodammodo omnia*. This formula implies and shows that there cannot be a complete heterogeneity between the real, whatever it be, and my thought. Rather it states that my intellect is capable by its very nature of knowing everything which exists. By its very nature it has an unlimited capacity, and to a certain extent it grasps the whole universe by a concept which is indeed confused but is still adequate.[10]

Inversely, everything which exists can be assimilated by thought and is accessible to thought as such. M. Le Roy was correct in stating that "anything beyond thought is unthinkable." But he made the mistake of taking this formula to be a justification of the idealist position. Anything outside thought is not only unthinkable but impossible, because being is the object of thought. Thought does not feed upon its own substance, but upon the real; and the real is by its very nature knowable or intelligible. Whether they spring from empiricist or idealist roots, all forms of absolute agnosticism are to be rejected because my intellect has an object which is absolutely unlimited.

At this point an objection naturally presents itself to the mind. Let us suppose that there is a being which is endowed only with sensation. Such a being would not know the limits of its own knowledge, and consequently it would not suspect

10. This might seem to suggest a metaphysical basis for the opinion that every created intelligence has a natural desire for the beatific vision. It is true that each such intelligence has by its very nature an unlimited curiosity. That nature is, however, finite. Consequently, no created intelligence has a natural right to or any natural possibility of acquiring an intuition of the infinite and transcendent Being. The beatific vision, therefore, can only be a supernatural gift gratuitously bestowed by God.

the existence of any knowledge higher than sensation. But are we not in exactly the same condition regarding a knowledge which might be higher than intellection?

The solution to this difficulty emphasizes once more the absolute value of thought. The organic character of pure sensation limits it by its very nature to spatio-temporal experience. If the animal were conscious of his activity, he would be conscious of the natural limits of his knowledge. But since intellection has for its formal object *being,* that is, an absolute value which is opposed only to non-being, then intellection is a kind of knowledge which is *by its very nature unlimited.* And since intelligence necessarily implies self-consciousness, then the intelligent subject knows that he has an unlimited capacity and he realizes that any apparent limitation to his knowledge is only specious (non-being is only a specious limitation of being). Considered as experience, our complete human knowledge is limited to our sensation and personal experience. But because man's intellect surpasses all limits by its transcendental capacity, man is aware of those limits. Consequently, we can conceive the possibility of a higher degree of intellection than our own (for example, a thought which would not be bound to experience and would not depend upon a datum) ; but we must positively exclude the possibility of any kind of knowledge which would be superior to intellection itself.

What relation is there between the intelligibility of a being and its possibility? Some treatises on metaphysics devote a great deal of attention to the "possibles." The possible is ordinarily defined as "that which does not exist, but which can exist." Authors then distinguish between the intrinsic and extrinsic possibility of the possibles. The extrinsic possibility of a being means that a cause exists which can produce this being; extrinsic possibility is also called relative possibility (that is, it is relative to the cause), or positive possibility (for the cause explains in a real and positive way how the effect is possible). The intrinsic possibility of a thing means that the elements which define or constitute it do not contradict one another. It is also called absolute possibility (because it is a property of the thing itself, apart from any relation to a cause), or negative possibility (the absence of contradiction is obviously a negative property).[11] Thus authors will say that a "house of gold" has extrinsic possibility if an artisan exists who can construct it; it has intrinsic possibility if the elements ("house" and "gold") which constitute it do not exclude one another, as they would exclude one another in the case of the "squared circle."

Certain authors hold that the intelligibility of a thing is the same as its intrinsic possibility. We have already stated that the concept of possibility is a highly complex notion which should be defined in terms of a previously developed theory of becoming and contingency. We have also noted that the possible can be known only through the actually existing thing. For these two reasons, the question of possibility should not be raised at this time when treating intelligibility. If these authors still insist on linking possibility and intelligibility, then we are obliged to state that the solution proposed does not seem quite acceptable. As a matter of fact, in metaphysics we cannot separate intrinsic and extrinsic possibility because the one necessarily implies the other. If we have shown that a cause exists which can produce a certain being, then that very fact implies that this being is not

11. The expression "negative possibility" is sometimes employed in a quite different and rather improper sense as referring to an object which we do not grasp as either possible or impossible. Thus, for example, in theology authors speak about the negative possibility of mysteries such as the Trinity, the Incarnation, and so forth.

contradictory in itself. Likewise if we have shown that a being is intrinsically possible, then this means that it is not contradictory for that being to exist. Now it would be contradictory for it to exist if no cause existed capable of producing it. In other words, we must stress the point that metaphysics can never be satisfied with a partial abstract point of view; it must consider the object in its concrete existence as a complete reality. From this point of view, extrinsic and intrinsic possibility always imply each other: the two possibilities merge on the metaphysical level. Consequently, it is the total possibility, both extrinsic and intrinsic, which should be linked with intelligibility. Everything which is, is intelligible or true, and possible.

That which is, can be. *Ab esse ad posse valet illatio;* and, we might add, *et ab esse tantum.* We know that beings are possible only by their actual existence and by the actual existence of their causes. Consequently, the ideal order of Plato, the eternal truths of Augustine, the order of essences and possibles of Suarez and many modern scholastics, have solidity only by virtue of the concrete real order. Ontology must be built upon the solid basis of the existent thing.

§ 6. Desirability

Every being is desirable or good in so far as it exists.

A final relation of agreement essential to every being appears when we compare any being with the intellectual appetite or will. Our analysis of consciousness has shown that knowledge is only one part of man's total activity. Knowledge is accompanied by our appetite or faculty of enjoyment, and just as the knowing activity implies a spiritual element, or thought, so the appetite implies a spiritual element correlative to thought. This is the will. The perfect act of the will consists in "enjoyment" following upon the "possession" of being by the intellect. The imperfect act of the will consists in the "tendency" or "desire" directed toward the same object.[12] Once we have defined the will as the intellectual appetite, a very simple reflection suffices to show us the relation of agreement existing between every being as such and the will.

Major: Everything which exists is intelligible.

Minor: That which is intelligible forms the object of my intellectual appetite or will.

Conclusion: Everything which exists forms the object of my will: it is intellectually desirable, likeable, or lovable. It is a source of intellectual enjoyment. In short, everything which exists is good in so far as it is being.

We can trace this process of deduction very easily: (a) the affirmation of *being;* (b) the search for an *extrinsic relation of agreement;* (c) the affirmation of the intellectual appetite or the *will;* (d) the discovery of the relation of *desirability,* appetibility, or goodness.

Here we are speaking about ontological goodness, or the goodness of being as such. It provides the ultimate foundation for moral goodness, that is, the goodness which affects the will and consists in the conformity of the will to the real order, and the submission of the free will to the natural requirements of the ontological order.

The meaning of the thesis which we have just proved parallels the meaning of the preceding thesis very closely: every being is desirable in the measure in which it is intelligible, since the relation of being to my will is measured by its relation to my intellect. My will derives pleasure from

12. Van Steenberghen, *op. cit.,* pp. 154-56.

the being which is possessed by my intellect. It enjoys every-thing which my intellect knows. In this thesis we do not affirm that my will finds a distinct joy in every existing thing; rather we affirm that it enjoys the universal order which is known by my intellect in a confused way at least.

Every being is desirable or good in so far as it exists. Here again the later developments of philosophy will bring out the rich implications of this principle.

Some authors link up ontological goodness with perfec-tion, or even with activity. They say that every being is desirable or appetible in so far as it is "perfect" and in so far as it is a "source of activity." These expressions, how-ever, do not seem to be either exact or suitable at this time. They do not seem to be exact because the reason why a being is desirable should be sought for in the very being of the thing, and nowhere else. A being is good precisely because it exists. These expressions should not be used at this time because the concepts of "perfection" and "activity" are far too complex to be employed at the beginning of metaphysics. We will meet these notions later when we study finite beings.

Having completed in this way the list of extrinsic rela-tions of agreement, we should now examine the relations of agreement which are intrinsic to every being. But as we have already said, there is only one relation of this sort, and it is a relation of pure reason, namely, the identity of every being with itself. A relation of pure reason elicits little in-terest in metaphysics.

§ 7. Conclusions

We can draw several conclusions from our derivation of the attributes of being.

1. *An Exhaustive Derivation.*—The list of derived attributes which we have proposed is exhaustive. There can be only five attributes of being because we have considered all the relations which can affect a being as being; the relations must be either intrinsic or extrinsic, relations of opposition or agreement.

2. *Comparison of this Complete Derivation of Attributes with the Derivation Proposed by St. Thomas.*—A brief examination of the way in which St. Thomas derives the attributes of being will help us see how complete our own derivation really is. To the same end we shall add a note on the problem of the beautiful.

In the well known passage of *De Veritate* (question 1, article 1), St. Thomas lists six transcendentals which have become classical in the Thomistic School: *ens, res vel essentia, aliquid, indivisum vel unum, verum, bonum.* Our process of derivation differs from that of St. Thomas on two points especially: *aliquid* and *res.*

We have substituted the term *distinct* or *determined* for the term *aliquid.* Here the difference is chiefly one of words. However, the term *aliquid* does have the disadvantage of implying the kind of opposition which one particular thing has to another particular thing, and hence it suggests the kind of distinction which is peculiar to a finite being when opposed to other finite beings.[13] To avoid this difficulty, some authors have proposed a disjunctive formula: *aliquid vel infinitum.* *Aliquid* would then signify the opposition peculiar to finite being; and *infinitum* would signify the opposition of unlimited being to non-being. We think that it is simpler and more exact to replace *aliquid* by *distinct* or

13. J. Webert (*Essai de métaphysique thomiste,* Paris, 1927, p. 70) did not apparently recognize this difficulty; his "some thing" is not genuinely transcendental.

determined. These terms can be applied equally well to both the finite and the infinite.

We believe that the transcendental *res* or *essentia* should be simply identified with *being.* For the distinction between being as "act" and being as "subject" is a purely grammatical distinction—at least at this stage of our study.[14]

When we try to give *essentia* a meaning distinct from that of being we find that we either come back to the idea of "determination" or "distinction," or we take *essentia* in the sense of "suchness" or "finite essence." But then we at once leave the sphere of the transcendentals. In our derivation of the transcendentals *essentia* was replaced by ontological *similarity.* This attribute was not seen by St. Thomas.

3. *The Problem of the Beautiful.*—Is not the beautiful also an attribute of being as such? Some deny that it is because they hold that beauty implies order, harmony, and consequently variety or diversity. According to this opinion, the beautiful is an attribute of the finite world, particularly of the material world. Others say that beauty is an attribute of being because beauty is the same as "the goodness of truth" *(splendor veri).* The beautiful would be the true in so far as desirable or appetible.

We believe that both these views are wrong. The first view errs by refusing to attach the beautiful to the supreme values, that is, to the metaphysical values. The second view errs by failing to see that, on the metaphysical level, the beautiful is *identified* with the good and therefore does not constitute an attribute distinct from the desirability of being.

In fact, on the metaphysical level, the desirability of being as known or thought is the same as the desirability of being in itself. Desirability or goodness is the relation of

14. See above, chap. 1, § 2, n. 3.

agreement of a being with an appetite or capacity of enjoyment. Now there is only one appetite directed toward being as such, because intellection is the only way of possessing being as such, and to intellection corresponds the intellectual appetite. Consequently, there is only one relation of desirability in being as such. When we consider the *complete* human appetite, we can distinguish an order of the good and an order of the beautiful, because man can "possess" a material object either by taking it for himself or by contemplating it. He can derive enjoyment either from his physical possession of the object or from his knowledge of it. In this way the object can have a value of "goodness" or a value of "beauty" for him. But these categories disappear on the metaphysical level. We must therefore admit that ontological goodness is the ultimate foundation for all the more particular human values such as the virtuous *(honestum),* the useful *(utile),* the pleasant *(delectabile),* and the beautiful (pulchrum).

4. *These Attributes are not New Realities.*—When we consider the attributes of being in themselves they are identical with being. We have already noted that the attributes of being are not realities distinct from being itself. Consequently, they are not "properties" in the strict sense of the term. The *proprium,* which is the fourth of the five predicables listed in formal logic *(genus, differentia, species, proprium, accidens),* indicates a determination which necessarily belongs to the essence of a subject, but which remains extrinsic to it. It is in this sense that the intellect is said to be a property of human nature.

When we speak of the attributes of being, the term "property" is taken in a broader sense to mean "that which necessarily belongs to," or "that which should be predicated of."

St. Thomas calls these attributes *passiones entis* (because they "affect" being logically), or *modi generales entis,* or *transcendentia.*

5. *These Attributes are New Concepts.*—When we consider the attributes of being as expressed in concepts, then they are new concepts distinct from the concept of being. They mark a certain progress in our knowledge of being, because they bring out the relations which affect being and constitute new intelligible aspects of it. We can summarize this advance in our reasoning in the following way:

being + relation of opposition + non-being = distinct.
being + relation of opposition + multiple = undivided.
being + relation of agreement + being = similar.
being + relation of agreement + intellect = intelligible.
being + relation of agreement + will = desirable.

Since these new concepts express the real just as adequately as the concept of being, they will have the same logical properties as the concept of being itself: they are *analogical* in their meaning; they are *transcendental* in their extension; they are *convertible* with the concept of being, and convertible among themselves. *Ens, unum, verum, bonum convertuntur.*

This convertibility of the transcendental concepts furnishes me with a new series of metaphysical principles: that which is *distinct,* is being, undivided, similar, intelligible, and desirable; that which is *undivided,* is being, distinct, similar, intelligible, and desirable; that which is *similar* is being, distinct, undivided, intelligible, and desirable; that which is *intelligible* is being, distinct, undivided, similar, and desirable; that which is *desirable* is being, distinct, undivided, similar, and intelligible.

Finally, to deny the attributes of being is equivalent to denying being itself; it is equivalent to non-being.

The *non-distinct,* the *indistinct,* or the *indeterminate* cannot exist as such. That which is, in so far as it is, cannot be indistinct or undetermined. Consequently, if we meet indetermination in reality (in matter, for example), the problem thus raised must be solved by showing that it is, in fact, a case of relative indetermination, and that it can be reconciled with the determination had by being as being.

The *non-undivided,* that is, the *divided* or *multiple,* cannot exist as such. That which is, in so far as it is, cannot be divided or multiple. Consequently, every case of division, every case of internal multiplicity, and every case of composition that we find in reality, raises a metaphysical problem. We must show that composition can be reconciled with the essential unity of every being as being.

The *non-similar* or *dissimilar* cannot exist as such. That which is, in so far as it is, cannot be dissimilar. Consequently, every case of opposition between beings raises a problem, because it must be reconciled with the essential similarity of all beings as existing.

The *non-intelligible,* the *unthinkable,* or the ontologically "false" does not exist. That which is, in so far as it is, cannot be unintelligible or false. It is only from certain incomplete and partial points of view that the real can appear unintelligible. For example, it may happen that the real is not fully intelligible for a certain kind of intellect. It may be that a reality is not intelligible by itself, but must be referred to some other thing. We can find applications of this metaphysical principle even in the most commonplace expressions. Thus a "false" diamond is simply not a diamond; a "false" piece of gold is simply not a piece of gold. This counterfeit coin is of such a nature that it can derange my judgment and lead me to say that it is something which it is not. Not being gold, it is not "intelligible" or affirmable as gold. We can also note that in this case the falsity is completely relative, because that which is a false diamond is a piece of genuine glass, and that which is a false piece of gold is a piece of authentic copper.

Finally, the *non-desirable,* the *non-good,* or the ontologically *evil,* does not exist. That which exists cannot be evil as such. If evil does exist, then, it can never be absolute evil. It will always consist in the privation of some particular good. We still have to explain how that is possible. In any case the foundations of *absolute pessimism* are destroyed, because being as such cannot be evil; that is, it cannot be the source of displeasure or suffering for the will. Manichean *dualism* is also excluded, for evil cannot be a first principle in the way that the good is. That would amount to saying that non-being was an absolute entity opposing being.

Part Two

THE ORDER OF FINITE BEINGS

IF THE reality given in my experience presented only the face of being or reality, then our ontology would terminate at this point. Being would appear to me to be perfectly distinct or determined, undivided, intelligible, and desirable, and no further question would be raised in this regard. This being would impose itself of itself because, opposed only to non-being, it would not be conditioned by anything.[1]

But the reality which offers itself to me is not as simple as that. The attributes of being generate a whole series of problems for the metaphysician because experience raises difficulties concerning each of them. Let us take any object at all; this dog, for example, in so far as it exists, is opposed only to non-being. Consequently, it is perfectly *distinct* or perfectly *determined*. But in addition, it is also opposed to something besides non-being because it is opposed to myself, to this table, to other dogs; in brief, it is opposed to all the realities which surround it. In that sense it is no longer perfectly and absolutely distinct, because it is *determinable*. It becomes other, it communicates with other things (by breathing, eating, perceiving, and so forth). In so far as it exists, this dog is perfectly *one* or *undivided;* yet it is *composed* of parts, it can be dissected, it is to some extent multiple. It is *similar* to every other being; yet in so far as it is *such* a being, it is opposed to every other being. I suddenly realize that the dog is no longer fully *intelligible;* it

1. Such a hypothesis would exclude any ontological similarity which implies a multiplicity of beings.

70

has become a mystery for me. Some aspects of its being have become paradoxical and unintelligible. It is no longer so desirable for the mind. It has become a source of unrest and annoyance for the intellectual appetite or will.

Obviously, all these difficulties spring from the existence of diversity, multiplicity, and oppositions within being, from the modalities of being or the determinations which mutually exclude one another and which break the unity of the real. In short, they come from the cases of opposition which we see among finite beings. Here we face a new problem: how can we explain diversity in terms of being? How can being be multiple, while remaining one? How can we explain that this existent thing is opposed to not only non-existent things, but also to that existent thing? This problem will give rise to very complicated inquiries, and far from being completed, ontology will now reveal some surprising developments.

Chapter I

PLURALISM

From the very beginning of man's philosophical reflection, the existence of the multiple has proven a scandal for metaphysicians. This paradox of the one and the many is had in every object which is opposed to other objects and does not identify itself with the rest. This object is entirely "being," from which point of view it is not opposed to anything. This object is entirely "such," from which point of view it is opposed to all the rest. How can this be possible?

We could, of course, content ourselves with merely noting that there is diversity in being. Strictly speaking, men are not obligated to grapple with the problem raised by this fact nor to interest themselves in it. But this is no justification for stating that the problem does not exist.

Before trying to solve the problem, we will state the question more precisely by showing how diversity actually presents itself to us in our own experience.

§ 1. Our Experience of the Multiple

From the very beginning the universe appears to common sense and to the man in the street as a kind of *order of finite individuals,* human persons, animals, plants, inanimate beings. Here we are using the term *individual* in its traditional sense *(indivisum in se et divisum ab alio).* An individual is a being which is undivided in itself and distinct from every other. It is therefore a being characterized by two fundamental attributes, distinction and indivision, autonomy and unity. The finite individual is one which opposes itself to other individuals, one whose reality is extraneous to that of other individuals, one whose perfection is limited by other perfections extrinsic to its own. Now the beings which common sense distinguishes in the universe meet these conditions. Each of these beings is opposed to all the others; each possesses a certain unity and autonomy even though each one also reveals a more or less basic dependence on the rest. As a matter of fact, this view of common sense is not as naïve as it might appear at first sight. It results from an interpretation; it is the fruit of a long experience. It involves a complete elementary philosophy, for common sense does not at all believe that every "such reality" is a "finite individual." For example, it does not believe that the eye, the stomach, and the oak leaf are individuals; rather it takes them to be "parts" of individuals, or "organs" belonging to individuals. Again, common sense believes that the intellect and will are not individuals even though we can oppose them as one object to another. The primitive may think that the aeroplane flying over the jungle is an individual and even a living individual; but the civilized man knows that the aeroplane, the clock, and the printing press are only artificial realities which do not have genuine internal unity. On the other hand, the civilized man may perhaps consider the crystal to be a genuine individual because it possesses a natural structure; or he may say that a fallen apple is an individual. Here the apple's internal organization is even more remarkable than that of the crystal. In brief, the man in the street tries to weigh the objects he experiences to determine which ones are genuine individuals, that is, realities possessing a true autonomy and unity.

Positive science forces common sense to modify its views in some respects. Thus science looks on the fruit which has fallen from the tree as merely a portion of matter separated from the living individual, and therefore lacking true organic unity. On the other hand, science holds that the seeds contained in ripe fruit (the kernels and stones) are new individuals. These seeds contain potentially new representatives of the species. Science supports the common-sense view regarding men, animals, and plants because it recognizes that they are genuine biological individuals.[1] Science refuses to decide in the case of the crystal, the molecule, the atom, because it is impossible to tell with any certitude just where the individual is to be found in the inorganic material world. Should we try to locate the individual in the world of the infinitely small, or should we look upon the entire cosmos as one great individual?

What stand should the metaphysician take in a situation of this sort? Should he take into consideration the opinions of common sense and the statements of positive science? Will he build his philosophy on these data? Should common sense be given its say in philosophical discussions? Let us make ourselves clear. Common sense cannot formulate philosophical laws in the strict sense, but it would be prudent for philosophers to heed it just as in olden times kings consulted their jesters. The judgments of common sense, and even more the views of scientists, can serve to draw the philosophers' attention to difficulties which might otherwise be overlooked. The suggestions of common sense and science will help the metaphysician get a better appreciation of the complexity of this problem of the diverse and will pro-

1. Sometimes it is as difficult to determine the true individuals in the biological world as it is to know whether the organism present is vegetal or animal. But difficulties of this kind represent "extreme cases" and do not discredit the general concept of individuality in biology. On this point, see D. Mercier, *Métaphysique Générale* (7th ed.; Louvain, 1923), pp. 96-102.

tect him against rash conclusions. In his turn the philosopher must evaluate these suggestions and determine standards for solution which are much more stringent than those of the scientist.

The metaphysician must try first of all to make the content of his own experience of the multiple more definite, and he must determine what elements of that experience can stand up under criticism. We see at once that our experience of the self is a privileged experience, because my consciousness of myself and of my own acts gives me an immediate and clear picture of my unity and autonomy—in short, of my own *individuality*. Let us examine this twofold characteristic somewhat more closely.

1. *Unity.*—I am aware that I am really "one" being, not "several." My activities may be most varied; my different tendencies may give rise to severe inner strain and struggle; my conscious life and biological organism may develop considerably; but still the unity of the self continues to dominate the multiplicity of my simultaneous and successive acts. The self is subject to a certain dispersion in space and time. The unity of the self triumphs over that condition also.

2. *Autonomy.*—I am aware that I am "distinct" from everything which surrounds me. This distinction is shown quite clearly by the way my body acts toward objects around it. My body changes position with respect to them; it has a life of its own. It reacts to its environment and tries to escape from the limitations of that environment in so far as it can. My spiritual activities and the immanent character of my thought and will give particular proof of my independence. In that case I am conscious that I myself determine the direction of my activities, without being necessitated by any physical force or by the motives which

present themselves to my mind, or even by some instinctive drive of my nature.

As far as my empirical knowledge can inform me, the self certainly possesses the characteristics of an individual. It therefore merits the name of *"person,"* if this term be taken to mean an individual capable of spiritual life, or an individual whose unity and autonomy have reached the perfection of spiritual consciousness.

Yet it is also obvious that the individuality of the self is not perfect. The self is complex and finite. What is implied in this twofold limitation?

3. *Complexity.*—We have already noted that this complexity of the self is caused by a twofold "dispersion" resembling dispersion in space and time. In the self we discover a number of factors which coexist and yet are mutually opposed. They constitute a greater or lesser threat to the internal unity of the person. Again, the person's permanent status is affected more or less profoundly by an increasing process of change.

4. *Finiteness.*—The self is characterized by its opposition to other things—just as one finite is opposed to other finite beings. But even though it is opposed to others, the self is still influenced by its environment and to a large extent depends on it. Consequently, it is subject to influence; it is "determinable"; its autonomy is not absolute; it depends on the beings which surround it. The limitations and needs of the self are shown most forcibly in the self's process of becoming or in its activity. First, this process of becoming reveals a need of growth or expansion. Secondly, this process of becoming is itself limited, restricted, subject to outside conditions, plagued by different obstacles.

The non-self is opposed to the self. The non-self obviously embraces a multitude of individuals more or less analogous to the self. In the corporeal world the philosopher can distinguish first of all other human persons similar to himself. For this he uses physiological similarities, characterisistics of conduct, and especially language, as criteria. The discovery of other resemblances which are more distant but still valid, justify his attributing the note of individuality to other living beings, to animals and plants. In this domain, however, individuality appears to grow weaker and weaker as we get further away from man, for the unity and autonomy diminish. In the material inorganic world, individuality evidently becomes extremely feeble. At any rate we find it impossible to determine with certitude, or even with a high degree of probability, just when true individuals are present on that level.

The world which I experience is, consequently, composed of a number of individuals which exist and evolve dependently on the material world. But are they really individuals in the metaphysical sense of the term, that is, beings which are multiple and individual, each of which possesses its own subsistence? We have seen that these individuals are not absolutely autonomous, that they depend on one another. Could it not be then that these individuals merely represent finite and multiple "modes," "parts," or "elements" of one unique being? Is it so completely and immediately evident that the hypothesis of Spinoza cannot be defended? Does it not seem to fit in better with the undeniable fact of universal solidarity?

Questions of this kind cannot be passed over in silence. We have to admit that the basic nature of the multiple does not reveal itself immediately to our minds. We cannot see directly the profound hidden bonds which unite beings among themselves. The decision between pantheism and pluralism, and between the different forms of pantheism and the different forms of pluralism, cannot be based on experience alone. We cannot decide immediately that the relative autonomy of certain individuals is a true ontological autonomy. We must be careful in even stating what the autonomy of the self or person means from a metaphysical point of view. For a simple reflection on my freedom will not show me the real scope of my independence as an active subject.[2] In short, at the moment when I begin my metaphysical investigation into the problem of the diverse, I cannot know in what sense and degree "finite individual beings" exist, or in what sense and degree the world of my experience is made up of a *plurality of beings* ontologically independent of each other.

We do not have to assume that they are, because *any kind of diversity* in being, even a superficial diversity, would suffice to raise the problem of the one and the many. We must explain how the diverse can exist. We shall see shortly that an adequate solution of this problem requires more precise data. But at this point it is not necessary to know whether the multiple individuals seen in our world of experience, subsist in themselves or subsist as "finite modalities" of one unique being; whether they subsist by themselves or in dependence on some cause. As used in our study of pluralism, the expressions "finite beings," "finite realities," "finite individuals," do not signify finite individual beings *each having its own proper subsistence* (for that would amount to assuming what is in question). Rather the terms simply signify realities which have a true internal unity and a true autonomy with respect to other realities from which

2. Not only am I not aware of enjoying absolute autonomy, but I am conscious that I depend on enviroment in my existence and in all activity, even in my voluntary activity. Furthermore, we shall show later that the finite will is not absolutely autonomous.

they are distinguished by opposition. This is so for men, animals, and plants. Leaving aside for the time being the question of whether these finite individuals may not be united by some deeper bonds, we shall first ask how they are possible *in themselves,* as they actually appear, that is, as finite modes of reality which are both similar in so far as *real,* and opposed in so far as *finite.*

In the course of time many attempts have been made to solve this problem. Some of the suggested solutions are extremist; others are more moderate. First, we shall show that the extremist solutions are futile, and we shall then develop the moderate solution which we think should be accepted.

§ 2. Absolute Monism

The first genuine metaphysicians proposed a radical solution which tries to solve the difficulty of the one and the many by simply suppressing the multiple, by denying the existence of diversity. Parmenides was the father of monism. In the modern period Spinoza was its most brilliant representative. His monism, however, was not an absolute monism, because it recognized a real plurality of modes in the one unique being.

It might seem that our earlier reflections concerning the object of metaphysics should incline us to a monistic conception of reality. For when we state that the concept of being is the adequate representation of the real and of all its determinations, we affirm that things in spite of their apparent diversity possess a fundamental unity. At that point we are very close to the position of radical monism. Radical monism holds that diversity is only apparent, superficial, and phenomenal; while the real is fundamentally one, undivided, indistinct, and unique, because *everything is being under every aspect.* Consequently, the concept of being would not be a truly universal concept, because it would represent one unique object.

This simple naïve form of radical monism cannot be defended, because it clashes with the evident and undeniable fact that diversity exists. We cannot simply suppress diversity, we have to explain it.

The monist declares that diversity is only an "appearance." Even so it would still be a real appearance and not simply non-being. But is diversity only a "superficial" reality? Perhaps, but even then it would still be a reality; and if diversity has any reality at all, it has metaphysical value and must be explained in terms of being.

In this case the monists may try to distinguish between appearance and reality, superficial reality and profound reality, the phenomenon and the thing in itself. Such distinctions are worthless here because all these classes come under being and express modes of being. Thus the "appearance" of diversity cannot be reduced to non-being pure and simple. It must be explained in terms of a real appearance, because non-being cannot pose as "diversity" to deceive me. Misinterpretations and mistakes are possible only when we are dealing with particular things. When we affirm the existence of reality as such, we can make no mistake because it is impossible to confuse being and non-being.

§ 3. *Absolute Pluralism*

Every reaction tends to swing to the opposite extreme. Since monism obviously fails to explain reality, some philosophers were inclined to accept the other extreme and deny all unity in the real. Diversity, they hold, forces itself upon me. This being is entirely opposed to that being; consequently, we cannot affirm that being is one. Reality is a pure multiplicity, an absolute diversity (phenomenalism). We may claim that the concept of being synthesizes the diversity, but that concept is only a label, a word, a *nomen* (nominalism), or at best a mental representation without objective value, an artifice of the mind to unify phenomena (conceptualism).

This is the viewpoint of absolute pluralism. It is perhaps true to say that absolute pluralism has never been defended in very thorough fashion. It represents rather the extreme form of a tendency revealed by every system which does not recognize the objective value of the concept of being. In antiquity absolute pluralism found its most typical representative in Heraclitus. The germs of absolute pluralism can be found in all the nominalist, phenomenalist, and empiricist philosophies.

Before evaluating the doctrine we must emphasize some of the implications of this radical point of view. It holds that the real universe is a confused mosaic of absolutes. No element of this universe has any intelligible relation or real similarity with any other element. Coexistence in space and the similarities which things apparently have among themselves, are due to pure chance and have no rational explanation. Consequently, the concept of being has no objective value. It is a purely artificial and entirely subjective mental representation. Finally, this view holds that the term "being" is completely equivocal. This attitude of absolute pluralism destroys intelligence because it denies the formal object of the intellect. It entails the total destruction of metaphysics because it destroys its object. Accordingly, it involves radical empiricism.

Both radical monism and absolute pluralism offer oversimplified solutions to the problem of the one and the many.

Instead of explaining the unity of the real, absolute pluralism arbitrarily suppresses it. Our criticism of radical pluralism consists essentially in restating the objective value of the concept of being; or in other words, in defending the formal object of the intellect and of metaphysics against the attacks of empiricism.

Absolute pluralism denies the intellect's affirmation of being, an affirmation which is basic, evident, and undeniable. For the affirmation of being necessarily implies the affirmation of the unity of being; we cannot deny the one without denying the other. When presented with any object whatever, my intellect conceives the idea of being as the adequate expression of that object and restores this idea to the object in a judgment of existence, affirming "that is." This judgment has a value which is immune from all illusion, confusion, and error, because being is not opposed to anything. Now this same judgment is formulated with the same objective evidence about any other datum. Consequently, the adequate expression of any object whatever coincides in a certain sense with the adequate expression of every other object. This means that all these objects are related among themselves by a basic similarity. We cannot deny this fundamental unity of the diverse without denying at the same time the affirmation of being, an affirmation which impresses itself upon us with overwhelming force.

At this point the empiricist will object that the concept of being, considered as a transcendental attribute, has a purely negative content. It signifies only opposition to non-being. It expresses a purely negative association among phenomena; what they have in common is simply that they are *not non-being*. Accordingly, this common note is strictly univocal, not analogical; it does not imply any true unity in the real.

This objection can be answered quite easily. Non-being is merely an artifice of the mind resulting from a denial of being. Consequently, the community of things which are not non-being, must be a community of *positive beings;* otherwise it would be a complete fiction. That alternative, however, would again involve absolute pluralism with all its disadvantages.

The empiricist still persists. He may admit that a thing must be something if it is not non-being, yet he holds that this positive element is the *essence,* quiddity, or determination proper to the object, that is, what distinguishes this object from every other. And he contends that this positive perfection does not imply any *community of positive perfection* or genuine resemblance. It is true that essences which are actually realized have something in common, that is, the state of existence, the fact of existence, the mode of actuality. But this raw "coexistence" does not constitute a positive perfection distinct from the perfection of the essences.

We must answer this objection by a global denial. This way of speaking runs counter to our intellect's most basic affirmations. There is only one positive perfection: *to be,* to be real, or to exist. Everything else is only a restriction, limitation, or modality of existence. Essence is a mode of existence, existence is not a mode of essence: *esse est actualitas omnis formae.*

The unity in diversity, or the real order which we see in the world of experience, helps us understand better the meaning of this metaphysical criticism of absolute pluralism. The positive sciences study the innumerable relations which phenomena manifest among themselves. These relations reveal a real *order,* that is, a unity in multiplicity, an order based upon all sorts of similarities, real affinities, and mutual reactions existing among the elements of the universe. This unity in diversity is shown even more clearly in the relations prevailing between the world of the multiple and my consciousness; since the multiple can be really assimilated and unified by my consciousness, it evidently constitutes an order of which my own consciousness is a part.

Thus we arrive at the following conclusion. The multiple contains within itself a real unity. The mind does not create this unity, it merely recognizes it. The affirmation of being shows me that a thing which is real cannot be completely foreign or completely other with respect to another reality. It is impossible for a thing to exist and yet have no relation at all to other existent things. The hypothesis that there might be several absolutes is unthinkable. I understand this, but I do not as yet have a full comprehension of it because the basic reason for it is still not clear to me. Furthermore, the nature of this mysterious unity in multiplicity is by no means clear to me. We shall try to gain more light on these matters as our inquiry develops.

§ 4. *Moderate Pluralism*

Thus we have excluded the two extremist solutions offered for the antinomy of unity and diversity in the real. How is that antinomy possible? How should we describe the situation?

Should we say that there is a *certain dosage* of unity in multiplicity? Should we describe the universe as a collection of opposed beings which are nevertheless similar? In that hypothesis the real becomes *simpliciter diversum secundum quid unum*. The aspect of multiplicity predominates over the aspect of unity. But then how can we explain the similarity of these different beings? Or should we say that there is a certain diversity in the unity? Should we look upon the real as being basically one, yet as being the source of a certain multiplication and the principle of different modalities? In this case the real would become *simpliciter unum et secundum quid diversum,* and primacy is accorded to the aspect of unity. But then how can the diverse come from the one?

Every suggested hypothesis merely raises an even more fundamental question; that is, what explains the possibility of the multiple? What constitutes the multiple in itself? How can this reality oppose itself to another reality while remaining entirely similar to it in so far as it is being? What does that imply? Finally, we must come back to the first problem: how can being be *multiple* without ceasing *to be?* The examination and solution of this problem will help us in our efforts to get a satisfactory picture of the universal order.

1. *Statement of the Problem: Analogy.*—What do we mean exactly by the doctrine of the *analogy of the concept of being?* Some writers think that the doctrine of analogy solves this paradox of the one and the many. But in reality, when we state that the concept of being is analogous, we are simply formulating the problem in a more precise way. We have not yet solved the problem at all. In fact, the irreducible indetermination of the concept of being merely expresses on the plane of human knowledge the twofold character of inseparable unity and diversity found in reality itself. Let us take two finite objects, this dog and this cat. If we consider them from the viewpoint of their partial determinations, by studying their generic and specific characteristics which serve as the basis for classifying abstract and universal concepts, then we should say that these two objects are *partially* similar (by the common genus "animal") and *par-*

tially different (by their respective specific differences). But if we consider them in their concrete reality, or in their true metaphysical value, then this dog and this cat cannot be analyzed in such a way. This individual dog is entirely comparable to that individual cat, because both are entirely "beings." Nevertheless, this dog and this cat are also entirely opposed to each other, because they are both entirely "such." [3] Consequently, this situation implies that the *concept* of being will be analogical, for since that concept represents adequately every concrete object, it must signify *indivisibly* the similarity and dissimilarity of this object with respect to every other object. The concept of being will have a meaning which is imperfectly one, proportional, and analogical. But what must the constitution of the real be in itself to provide an explanation for this twofold aspect of unity and diversity which my intellect sees? What is the ontological foundation for the analogy of the concept of being? These questions are still unanswered.

2. *The Constitutive Composition of the Finite Being.*— Here we reach a crucial step in our metaphysical inquiry. As our intellect struggles with the above paradox, it suddenly "discovers" that this situation means that the finite being manifesting this twofold characteristic *cannot be a simple reality.* It must be composed. It must imply some kind of real duality. For a reality which was simple could not tolerate the simultaneous predication of these two attributes—"entirely similar," "entirely dissimilar"—for such a predication would be hopelessly contradictory. If both affirmations referred to the same identical reality, one of them

3. Note that this point remains true in any and every hypothesis, whatever hidden bonds may unite ontologically these two objects of my experience. Considered in themselves, the two objects are completely similar and completely opposable.

would necessarily destroy the other. However, a compound reality could very well have irreducible characteristics, provided that these characteristics belonged to the object *by virtue of different, distinct components.* For in that case the two judgments attributing these characteristics to the same subject would not be contradictory; they would express that same subject entirely, but *under aspects which are really distinct.*

The analysis which we have just made can be put in the form of the following syllogism:

Major: A simple reality cannot be the subject of two irreducible attributes.

Minor: Every finite reality is the subject of two irreducible attributes.

Conclusion: A finite reality cannot be a simple reality.

The major of the syllogism becomes evident through a simple analysis of terms. For a being which was truly simple and excluded all duality could not assume two really irreducible aspects. A simple reality does not give rise of itself to a multiplicity of real aspects.

The minor merely repeats the statement of the paradox of the one and the many. We can formulate two judgments about every finite reality, that is, about every reality which is opposed to other realities. The predicates of these two judgments are absolutely irreducible, for one is the denial of the other. We can say that the finite is entirely *similar or comparable* as being to every other reality, and that it is entirely *dissimilar or opposable* as finite to every other reality.

Since the conclusion excludes simplicity from the finite being, it amounts to stating that the finite must involve a certain real duality, or a certain real composition.

As can be seen, the kernel of the proof is found in the *irreducible* character of these two attributes *(similar* and *dissimilar),* both of which express the same finite object. Now it is quite obvious that the same object can manifest different characteristics, when compared with various things. Thus the number 5 is at the same time "greater than 3" and "smaller than 7." In this case these two different aspects do not imply any duality in the number 5 itself, for the duality of aspects arises from the fact that the number 5 is being compared with two different objects. These two aspects are not irreducible since both result from the same nature of the number 5. However, different characteristics affect every finite being even when compared with the same object, that is, every other finite being. These predicated characteristics ("entirely similar," "entirely dissimilar") not only differ but mutually contradict one another; one excludes the other. Now if the finite being were simple, we would have to say that it was similar and dissimilar, comparable and opposable [4] *under the same aspect and at the same time.* In that case the judgments "This is not similar to that *in so far as finite,"* "This is similar to that *in so far as being,"* would be contradictory judgments, for the aspects *"in so far as finite"* and *"in so far as being"* would not be really distinct.

Before inquiring any further into the nature of this composition, we must examine critically the intellectual analysis involved in our demonstration.

This is the first time that we have employed the method of inference in our metaphysical analysis. This method transfers our analysis from the plane of immediate knowledge based on experience to the level of metaphysical impli-

4. Note that the expression "entirely" has no meaning if applied to a simple being, for no quality may be predicated of it in part.

cations, which are known only in a mediate and improper way through analogy with the objects of proper knowledge.

We give the name "immediate knowledge" to every knowledge which has a datum of experience for its object. The intellect then works on this immediate knowledge by its activity of reasoning in an attempt to bring out all the implications of that knowledge. But this analysis by reasoning can be developed in different ways. Thus our immediate knowledge of a triangle can give rise to a work of analysis, definition, and derivation of the properties of the triangle, as is done in geometry. We can develop our knowledge of a physical phenomenon by trying to discover the physical laws implied in the phenomenon. Metaphysics, because of its formal object, is always concerned with discovering the ontological conditions for the object of experience; in other words, the characteristics which enable us to describe it as being and which affect it as being. At this point we begin to see the fruitfulness of the principle of intelligibility: *ens est verum*. Every being is intelligible or conceivable. Every reality given must be capable of being assimilated by thought. It cannot give rise to contradictory affirmations. Consequently, we must recognize in every being, and affirm concerning every being, those ontological conditions without which it would become unintelligible, incoherent, and a source of contradictory affirmations.

Therefore, we must affirm of the finite being that it is not a simple reality, but that it entails a genuine internal composition. Now the object of this new affirmation is not known by any immediate knowledge, or as the term of human experience. We have only an improper knowledge of it by analogy with the objects of proper knowledge. We shall soon see that it cannot be represented by means of images borrowed from the data of our proper knowledge. Our human intellect can find no adequate representation for these metaphysical inferences.

Can we say anything further about the *nature* of this composition which we have discovered in finite beings?

Yes, but only what the principle of metaphysical inference authorizes. The meaning of the constitutive composition depends on its function of explaining the characteristics of the real as given in experience. Consequently, the composition is obviously not a composition *inter rem et rem,* that is, between two *autonomous* realities. (The family which is "composed" of two persons is an example of that type of composition.) A composition of this kind will not produce a genuine composite, since each component part still keeps its own autonomy and characteristics. If the finite being were composed of two independent realities, then the opposed characteristics which we have discovered in it would not belong to the same subject. Each characteristic would merely belong to one of the two juxtaposed parts.

The component parts of the finite being must, therefore, be conceived as *constitutive parts* of one single subject. In our experience we meet many objects which are composed of quantitative parts having different characteristics. Thus various organs go to make up the living being: an egg consists of a yellow nucleus and a whitish protoplasm; a rubber ball can be made of a red half and a blue half. Even though these quantitative parts combine to form one single object, they are united only *accidentally* and not essentially, because they can still exist independently and each one keeps its own characteristics. None of these compositions can serve as a model for the composition of the finite being because they simply would not explain the characteristic feature of the finite being—that it is both *entirely* similar and *entirely* opposed to every other. In the case of accidental compositions the characteristics of the parts affect the subject only partially not entirely. The organism is not entirely bony; the egg is not entirely yellow; the rubber ball is not entirely red, nor entirely blue.

Consequently, the compositions which we find in experience cannot serve as models of the ontological composition of the finite being. We are therefore obliged to postulate a much more intimate composition, but one which we can *no longer properly represent.* The component parts must be conceived as *essentially incomplete* and incapable of independent existence. They are correlative elements, real co-principles, "com-ponents," whose essential and indissoluble union produces the finite subject or "composite." Then, since the composite is only the synthesis of its component parts, the whole composite will share the nature of both the components. It will be entirely similar or comparable to every other reality by virtue of its *principle of similarity.* It will be entirely dissimilar or opposed to every other reality by virtue of its *principle of dissimilarity or diversity.*

A duality of correlative principles is unified by its very nature. There is no need to stress this point. The finite being is a real synthesis, or real compromise, of its co-principles. Each principle exists only *with* the other, *by* the other, *for* the other. It is this indissoluble unity which explains the surprising characteristics of the composite in which are harmonized and reconciled the most paradoxical attributes. It explains the irreducible analogy of the notion of being and its imperfect and proportional unity which defies all analysis. If the notion of being expresses *at the same time* that which unites and that which opposes, the similar and the diverse, it is precisely because the finite being is really a compromise of the one and the other.

We must now try to fix the terminology to be used in

describing this composition of the finite and its two component parts. This real composition on which analogy is based
should be called the *constitutive composition* of the finite
being. This composition makes the finite reality a being,
and gives it a place in the community of beings. This is the
most exact name for the composition.

What names should we give to the two component elements of the finite being? If we keep in mind the problem
which this composition tries to solve, then the following
names will be most exact: one principle should be called the
*principle of similarity, community, participation in the
whole, unity* (since it is by reason of this principle that the
finite being is inscribed in the universe and is attached to
the absolute); the other principle should be termed the *principle of dissimilarity, suchness or finiteness, isolation, measure, restriction, diversity* (since it is by reason of this second
principle that the finite being is opposed to every other being
and restricted within the limits of its own suchness.)

The traditional names usually applied to the components
have the advantage of being briefer, but they involve serious drawbacks. They may be used, provided that we understand the exact sense in which they are taken.

Thus it is obvious that the terminology *(quod est* and *quo
est)* which the thirteenth century adopted from Boethius
is very ambiguous, because we tend to translate *quod est* by
"that which is," and consequently to consider that principle
as if it were a subsistent subject and not a principle of being
or a *principium quo.* We should translate *quo est* as "that
by which the composite is," and *quod est* as "that which the
composite is," or its *taleity.* Besides it would be more exact
to substitute *quo est tale* ("that by which the finite being is
such") for *quod est.*

Even the expression *quo est* itself is not without its drawbacks, because the principle of similarity cannot be called "principle of being" without further ado. For if it were simply the "principle of being," then the other principle could only be "the principle of non-being," which is not exact. Indeed, our discovery of the constitutive composition shows us a first "division of being," or two basic "modes" of being: the principle of similarity represents the *perfect mode,* and the principle of diversity represents the *imperfect mode* of being. Radical monism recognizes only the distinction "being and non-being," but there is also room for the distinction between "the perfect and the imperfect," or "fullness of being and measure of being." Because of its component parts the finite reality participates in both these modes. The finite reality is not properly a synthesis of a principle of being and a principle of taleity; in a stricter sense, it is a synthesis of a principle of perfect being and a principle of imperfect being or taleity.

The terms *esse* and *essentia* (being and essence, existence and essence) have, besides the disadvantages noted above, the added defect of using abstract terms to indicate concrete elements (that is, the component parts of the finite being). Too often these abstract terms keep their abstract signification in philosophical language. Thus, for example, when we say "Existence is a logical accident," (here we are speaking about the quality of existence); or when we say "Corporeity is part of the essence of man," (here "essence" is equivalent to definition, or nature); it is evident that the terms "essence" and "existence" are being taken in an abstract sense, which is, in fact, the first sense in which these terms are employed.

What is the relation between this constitutive composition and the doctrine of act and potency?

Aristotle employed the doctrine of act and potency to

explain the fact of becoming. The potency-act doctrine was developed independently of the metaphysical problem which we are now considering. The Middle Ages gave a broader meaning to the terms "act" and "potency." Philosophers began to look upon the composition of *essentia* and *esse* as a particular instance of the potency-act relation. Within a short time the perspective had altered so much that thinkers began to use the metaphysical principles relating to act and potency, and especially the principle *Actus non limitatur nisi per potentiam subjectivam realiter distinctam,* to prove the composition of *esse* and *essentia.*

In a systematic metaphysics, however, we should not use the doctrine of act and potency until we take up the problem of becoming. Consequently, we postpone this question of the relationship between the act-potency doctrine and the constitutive composition of the finite being until later.

The controversy concerning the distinction of essence and existence in finite things has gone on for centuries. There is little likelihood of quick settlement. This seems to be due very largely to the historical circumstances surrounding the development of the doctrine of the real composition. Aristotle and perhaps Boethius had caught glimpses of this doctrine; Greek Neoplatonism taught it and Arab Neoplatonism had adopted it. This doctrine of the distinction between essence and existence became the central doctrine in the metaphysics of Avicenna, who handed it on to Latin scholasticism in the thirteenth century. Yet we can say that this doctrine affords a typical example of how a philosophical problem can be badly put and, as a consequence, badly solved. Only after interminable discussion were the necessary revisions gradually made. Many philosophers fervently defended the important truth implied in this thesis of the real composition, but their presentation of the thesis caused a very legitimate distrust of it in the minds of many others.

At this point we do not have to retrace the history of these controversies, nor do we have to answer the many different kinds of difficulties which have been formulated against the doctrine of the real composition. Any such examination would exceed the scope of our treatise. A few brief remarks must suffice.

For the most part the classical objections to the thesis do not affect our position, for from our point of view they have only an historical interest. At first sight, the only difficulties that could affect our view are the Suarezian objections based on a consideration of the nature of the two principles taken separately. But let us note that the principle of intelligibility, *ens est verum,* refutes the point of view basic to objections of this sort. A thing is intelligible in so far as it exists. Now the co-principles do not exist separately, they exist by each other and for each other. Taken separately, they are neither conceivable nor intelligible, and every objection which implies that they are is irrelevant.[5]

To conclude, then, moderate pluralism solves the antinomy of the one and the many and explains the analogy of the concept of being in terms of the constitutive composition of the finite being. This constitutive composition is a *metaphysical inference* arrived at by metaphysical analysis. It lies outside the scope of our proper knowledge, and for this

5. On the history of the problem of the real composition, see L. De Raeymaeker, *Metaphysica Generalis* (2nd ed.; Louvain, 1935), II, pp. 323-47; *Philosophie de l'être* (Louvain, 1946), pp. 123-55. These two works also provide a sufficient bibliography of the subject. I have treated the question myself in the following places: "La composition constitutive de l'être fini," *Revue Néoscolastique de Philosophie,* November, 1938, pp. 489-518; "La littérature thomiste récente," *Ibid.,* November, 1939, pp. 601-605; *Siger de Brabant d'après ses oeuvres inédites* (Louvain, 1942), II, pp. 590-601.

reason it remains mysterious. Further along in metaphysics we shall see the root reason for its mysterious character. Our knowledge of this composition is so imperfect that it prevents us from deducing or inferring anything from it. In this sense the theory is not directly productive. However, the insight which it gives us into the basic conditions of finite being will throw a great deal of light on the further development of metaphysics and will give added meaning to future theories.

3. *The Relative Character of the Finite Being.*—The very possibility of finite being and of any multiplicity of finite beings opposing one another depends then on this constitutive composition as an intrinsic requirement. Looked at in the light of this first metaphysical law, the world of the multiple now appears to be a collection of composed realities which are similar to each other by virtue of their principle of perfection, and different from each other by virtue of their principle of limitation.

It is quite true that this first part of our answer to the problem of the multiple is not completely satisfying, because it does not fully explain the *unity* seen in the multiple. Up to this point the paradox of the one and the multiple has been resolved rather in favor of the multiple, because the finite beings are *simpliciter diversa* (they oppose one another, are completely foreign to each other), and only *secundum quid unum* (by virtue of their ontological similarity). Now how is it that these opposed realities can be similar? How and why can realities foreign to each other still possess an internal principle of similarity? Are they, indeed, really foreign to each other?

Questions of this sort help us discover another metaphysical law: "Every finite being is a caused being." This law expresses the *extrinsic* condition needed to make finite beings possible.

For the first time in metaphysics we meet a law which appeals to an extrinsic influence to explain some characteristic of the finite being, or to make it intelligible. This law states that the similarity of the finite being to other beings implies a causal dependence; it states that the finite being is similar in its very being, or as being, because it is conditioned or caused in its very being.

The proof of this law rests upon the *principle of causality*, which we meet here for the first time. This principle can be formulated in several ways: "That which does not exist by itself, exists by something other than itself"; "That which is not intelligible by itself, is intelligible by something other than itself." Or again: "That which is not unconditioned, is conditioned by something"; "That which is not absolute, is relative to something"; or finally, "That which does not exist by itself, depends on an extrinsic cause."

A reality which is in any way the reason for the existence of another reality, is called a *cause*. Authors distinguish intrinsic causes and extrinsic causes. The component parts or co-principles from which the being is formed are termed the intrinsic or constitutive causes of the being. The extrinsic causes of a being refer to realities distinct from this being which exercise some influence on its constitution or development. The name extrinsic cause properly belongs to the efficient cause, since this cause exercises a real influence on another reality. The exemplary cause and final cause are termed causes only in a wider and less proper sense. Thus when an intelligent efficient cause exercises its influence to produce a determined effect, we call the object which serves as a model for the realization of that effect the "exemplary cause," and we call the goal which the intelligent agent wishes to realize by his causality, the "final cause." Consequently, the exemplary and final causes have no direct influence on the effect. Their influence on the mind of the efficient cause belongs to the intentional order.[6]

The formulas of the principle of causality given above obviously refer to the extrinsic cause properly speaking, or the efficient cause. The principle states that a reality whose existence and intelligibility are not self-explanatory must depend in some way on an extrinsic reality or efficient cause.

The principle of causality is evident by virtue of the principle of the excluded middle. Every being which exists must exist either by itself or by something other than itself; it must be either unconditioned or conditioned, absolute or relative, independent or dependent on a cause. There is no other possible alternative.[7]

Kant's views on causality have caused lengthy discussions among scholastics as to whether the principle of causality

6. The intentional order is the order of knowledge as such; the exemplary cause and the final cause exercise their influence through the medium of knowledge by directing the intelligence of the efficient cause.

7. A. Grégoire in *Immanence et transcendance* (Bruxelles-Paris, 1939, p. 87), suggests a possible alternative. The terms "to be by oneself" and "to be by another" are both positive terms and not opposed as contradictories. Between them we could logically introduce a middle term— "to be neither by oneself nor by another." Grégoire, however, here seems guilty of equivocation, for the two terms actually are opposed as contradictories. "To be by another" means "to be under the influence of another"; but "to be by oneself" does not mean "to be under the influence of oneself" anymore than the phrase "to be by essence" means "to be by virtue of one's essence," which would be tantamount to imagining that a being could be its own cause. "To be by oneself" really means "to be without depending on another." Thus we see that the term "to depend on another" or "to be by another" is in reality contradictory to the term "not to depend on another" or "not to be by another." So also the phrase "to exist by essence or essentially" really means "to exist without needing something else for one's existence." This phrase has the same meaning as "to be by oneself." Consequently, Grégoire's hypothesis "to be neither by oneself or by another" (p.87) is logically incoherent and metaphysically impossible.

should be said to be analytic or synthetic. In Kantian terminology a judgment is called analytic when the predicate is
contained in the essence of the subject, and can therefore
be discovered by a simple logical analysis of that subject.
In the contrary case the judgment is termed synthetic.
When the terms are defined in this way, it can be readily
seen that *the principle of causality is an analytic principle,*
provided that the subject (of the principle) is taken in its
complete ontological value, that is, as being. Indeed when a
thing which does not exist by itself is examined from the
viewpoint of being, then we see that the thing's relation
of dependence to a cause forms a part of its very nature, or
is essential to it. It is true that the cause as such remains
extrinsic to the being which does not exist by itself, but that
being has an intrinsic and essential relation to the cause.
This relation is implied in the ontological nature of that
being as an absolutely necessary condition to such an extent
that it would be contradictory to affirm that this being existed and yet deny that it was caused.[8]

Having thus established the value of the principle of
causality when taken in a very broad sense, we can now
reason as follows:

Major: That which is not intelligible by itself must be
explained by something other than itself.

Minor: A finite being which is similar to other finite
beings is not intelligible by itself.

8. Consequently, I cannot accept the view of Father Grégoire (*op. cit.,*
p. 85). "We may," he writes, "push our analysis of the concept of any
finite being whatever as far as we can, but we will not discover the
concept of cause in it, or even of a relation to a cause." On the contrary,
I believe that the analysis of the *metaphysical concept* of the finite being
leads us directly to the discovery of a relation to a cause. Furthermore,
we see that this relation forms part of the very essence of the finite
being as such: finite being = similar being = being which is relative to
something else.

Conclusion: A finite being which is similar to others must be explained by something other than itself.

The principle of causality serves as the major of the argument.

The minor merely repeats the difficulty we encountered previously. A finite being is a being which is opposed to other finite beings. It is a being whose distinctive reality is foreign to that of other finite beings. If we say that this being is similar to other finite beings of itself, this means either that we attribute this similarity to pure chance (in other words, we declare that it is unintelligible, after having defended it against absolute pluralism in the name of the principle of intelligibility), or we try to explain this similarity by saying that this finite being is the unique and adequate cause of all other beings. In that case the resemblance among finite beings would result from their participating in a common cause, and it would be adequately explained by that cause. But this explanation is excluded since far from precontaining other beings as their total cause, the finite being is completely opposed to them in so far as it is finite.

The conclusion states that the similarity of a finite object to others reveals a relation of dependence affecting the very being of the finite object. The similarity of one finite being to other beings can only be understood if that finite being is related to them by a causal bond of dependence. Only a causal relation can explain the "family likeness," or basic connaturality, evident among finite beings in spite of their mutual opposition.

Consequently, every finite being is a caused being. An *absolute finite being is a contradiction in terms.* As being, this thing would have to be related ontologically to all other beings by an adequate causal bond. And yet this bond could not be had, for this being could not be the adequate cause of others because it was itself finite, nor could it be caused itself since it was absolute.

We can sum up this analysis (contained in the commentary on the minor) in the following disjunctive syllogism:

Major: Every being which is similar to others is either a cause or is caused.

Minor: A finite being which is completely similar to other finite beings cannot be the cause of these others.

Conclusion: A finite being which is completely similar to other finite beings is caused.

At this point another objection naturally presents itself. Could not these resemblances seen in reality result from chance? At first sight this might seem to be possible: thus, for example, the fact that this wall and this piece of paper are both white hardly entails any relation or causal bond between the wall and the paper. We reply that this sort of resemblance can be called fortuitous or accidental, but only as long as we consider merely the proximate causes of the wall and paper. This point of view, however, is very superficial and incomplete. A qualitative similarity of this sort could not be explained unless it was rooted in the ontological similarity basic to all beings. And this basic similarity becomes intelligible only when explained by a causal bond among beings.

We might now attempt to give a more definite statement about the meaning and importance of this newly established law. We might try to determine better the nature of this "connection" or "causal bond" uniting finite beings. But after we get more information about the nature of the finite being, we shall be able to do this more intelligently and with more assurance. The examination of some additional facts will help us make important discoveries in this matter.

Chapter II

DYNAMISM

How can we further develop our knowledge of finite beings? We cannot rely exclusively on reasoning, since the obscurity of the constitutive composition prevents it from serving as a satisfactory starting point for further inference. We have to turn once again to the data of experience to make any further progress in our metaphysical analysis.

Now among the immediate and undeniable data of our experience we meet everywhere and continually one fact which is very closely linked to the fact of the diverse or multiple. This is the fact of *change* or *becoming,* or of *successive diversity.* And this fact poses a new problem similar to that raised by the one and the multiple. It is the problem of reconciling being (which seems to imply permanence) and becoming. What is becoming? How is it possible? How is it that that which is, can change?

After we first determine the significance of this new fact somewhat better, we shall try to discover the metaphysical laws involved in becoming.

§ 1. Our Experience of Change

We meet this undeniable fact of change both in our objective and in our subjective experience. Reality does not exist in a state of frozen immobility; it becomes other. The objects which I experience change their position, size, form, color, temperature, and so forth. I myself am continually developing in my knowledge, tendencies, and corporeal life.

We can sum up the descriptive analysis of change in the following points:

1. To be able to talk about change at all, we must be able to distinguish in some zone of our experience *two successive states which are not identical;* or in other words, a perceptible difference between a "before" and an "after." Every change, therefore, essentially involves two distinct termini, a starting point and an arrival point. Every change implies a successive diversity. On the phenomenal or empirical level, these two termini are not always both real. Consequently, we can distinguish three different types of change: (a) the passage from *non-being to being* (the "appearance" or "production" of a new object; for example, the appearance of a light or a sound); (b) the passage from *being to non-being* (the "disappearance" or "annihilation" of an object; for example, when a light is extinguished or a sound fades); (c) the passage from *one form of being to another form of being* (the "substitution" of one object for another; for example, when the water in a basin is changed into ice or steam, when a red light gives way to a green light). In the first two cases, only one of the terms of the change is real; the change itself is a radical one involving respectively the existence and non-existence of an object.

The fact that reality can be diverse has already caused difficulty. But that it can become other is even more perplexing. How can a thing which did not exist, begin to be? How can a thing which did exist, cease to be? How can one object substitute itself for another object? Why did the first object disappear and how? Why did the second object appear and how? Does anything of the first object remain in the second? Are there really three types of change in reality, as there seem to be, or is every change a transformation of one object into another? Or can all changes be reduced to cases of annihilation and creation?

2. Most changes are not instantaneous, but rather they involve a series of *intermediate states* between the two termini; thus, for example, in local motion, in the assimilation of food, in growth, in the gradual appearance or disappearance of a light, of a sound, and so forth. In these cases the problem of change becomes more complicated. What are these intermediaries? Can we count them? What binds them together? Still the presence of these intermediaries throws new light on the nature of these changes, because it shows that there is a certain continuity between the two terms, and it suggests the idea that one term is progressively "transformed" into the other.

3. Our experience with change also suggests that we can distinguish *two kinds of transformations* according as the subject examined is affected to a greater or lesser degree by the change. Some changes appear to be merely *superficial* modifications of the subject. A new determination affects the subject but does not destroy its identity. This seems to be the case when a billiard ball is set rolling, when a cat moves, grows, sleeps, awakens; when I think, walk, and feed myself. In these cases I become "other," without becoming "another." Other changes, on the contrary, seem to involve *profound radical* modifications of the subject even to the point of affecting its fundamental identity. This is the case with the cat which dies. Its identity seems to completely disappear and lose itself in the material world. But at this point we do not have to pass final judgment about the exact significance or legitimacy of this distinction.

4. On the level of the immediate data of experience we have definite knowledge only of the changes *which affect the self*. These changes are obviously transformations of the self

as the subject of the change. *I* feed myself, *I* grow, *I* walk, *I* desire, *I* suffer, *I* warm myself by the fire, *I* will one day die. Most of these transformations do not affect my personal identity. Hence they are not radical changes. But the last one (death) causes the destruction of my biological identity. It accordingly shows itself to be a much more fundamental transformation. It is clear of course that I personally have not yet had this supreme experience. But my observation of the consequences of death in my fellow men, supplements my personal experience.

These are the facts. How should we interpret them metaphysically?

The *metaphysical laws* of change will try to connect change to being and to express the ontological implications of the fact of change. For at first sight there seems to be a radical opposition between being and becoming, for "being" seems to imply permanence, while "becoming" or "change" obviously implies a denial of permanence.

Being implies permanence. Every being, in so far as it is being, is distinct or determined, since as being it is not opposed to anything. Since it is not opposed to anything, it excludes all otherness and cannot, then, as being become "other." The mere existence of a thing will never explain any change at all. The existence of a thing does not explain why the thing began to be, nor why it can cease to be, nor why it can become other. Consequently, a being does not change in so far as it is.

Nor is it true to say that a being changes because it is *such*. The suchness of a being can explain how it acquires determinations which it did not possess; it can become "other," because it was opposed to "another" thing. Nevertheless, the suchness cannot be the reason for this sort of change, for suchness is in itself a principle of determination and opposition. It is not because a thing is determined that it is determinable. It is not because a thing possesses a determination that it can lose it or acquire another.

Hence, whether we consider a being in its existence or in its suchness, every being seems to exclude becoming. Nevertheless, there is becoming in being. Reality changes. Yesterday it was not what it is today. It becomes other. The "before" is not identical with the "after." How can this be?

Here, as in the case of the paradox of the one and the many, extreme solutions have been proposed. We must first criticize these positions, and we shall then describe the view of moderate dynamism.

§ 2. Absolute Immobilism

Parmenides denied becoming, since he claimed that being is opposed only to non-being, and therefore being is not determinable. It is fully determined. To be is to remain identical with oneself and to be indeterminable. Becoming, then, is only an appearance, an illusion from which the philosopher must free himself.

We answer that this absolute immobilism is as inadmissible as absolute monism. Becoming is a fact which forces itself upon us with the same evidence as the multiple. If becoming is only an appearance, it has at least the reality of an appearance, and this point must be explained. If becoming is only an illusion, we must at least show how the illusion is possible, because non-being pure and simple cannot cause it. We cannot simply deny the fact of becoming; we must explain how it is possible.

§ 3. Evolutionism or Absolute Dynamism

This is the position taken by Heraclitus: "Everything passes away." In our times it has been taken up again by Henri Bergson and his disciples, especially Edouard Le Roy. For them becoming is the true reality: reality is evolution. To be is to become; the stable simply does not exist. It is our conceptualizing intellect which dissects becoming, analyses the creative evolution, pretends to stabilize the *élan vital* or the eruption of reality, and which automatically destroys it.

The prestige which Bergson enjoyed and the brilliant imagery which he used to present his doctrine should not deceive us concerning the true value of his position. Indeed, it seems that Bergson himself did not completely avoid the snares of conceptual thought, for "becoming" is also an abstraction. The concrete reality is, in fact, this acorn which becomes an oak, this child who becomes an old man, this human being who did not exist but exists today, this water which changes into ice. Or if we wish, the concrete reality is the whole material universe, which is today what it was not yesterday. In brief, the concrete real is a *subject* which changes, and which in order to change must exist, which in order to become "other" should first be "itself." It is, therefore, a subject which at every moment of its duration *is,* and is *determined,* while yet being *determinable.* But then the paradox reappears: how and why is the subject determinable? To refuse to put the problem in these terms is simply to refuse to think. Absolute evolutionism in fact belongs more to poetical imagination than to metaphysics, because it destroys the formal object of the intellect and of metaphysics itself. Bergson was a psychologist of genius and he has achieved fame enough there. We must not try to make a metaphysician of him.

§ 4. Moderate Dynamism

The genuine metaphysician will try to solve the antinomies seen in reality without sacrificing any element of reality. To exist implies duration or permanence, and yet the real changes. How can this fact be explained? Careful examination of the problem helps to discover two fundamental laws, one of which expresses the *intrinsic* condition for any becoming in the being which changes, the other of which expresses the *extrinsic* condition.

1. *Composition in the Dynamic Order.*—Every transformation implies that there is present in the subject which is transformed a principle of determinability which is essentially correlative to the principles of determination of this subject. In scholastic terms: *quidquid movetur habet in se potentiam subjectivam realem.*

Let us first explain the meaning of this principle. On the level of the immediate data of experience we have distinguished three types of apparent change: (a) the total *production* of an object; (b) the *disappearance* of an object; (c) the *substitution* of one object for another. This last type frequently presents itself as a more or less rapid *transformation* of one and the same reality, which passes from state A to state B. What interpretation should we give to these phenomena?

The only changes whose inner nature we can grasp immediately, at least to some extent, are those which affect the self. All such changes are more or less profound transformations of the self. Then by analogy with what takes

place in myself, I can form some idea of similar changes
taking place around me, in men, animals, and plants. Transformations take place, then, in the world of my experience.
But, at least for the present, I cannot say whether there may
actually be any other kinds of change.

The metaphysical law which we have just enunciated is
concerned with these transformations. It expresses the
intrinsic condition implied in every change of this kind.
It affirms that every transformation reveals a dynamic composition between a principle of determinability, or "potency,"
and the principles of determination, or permanence, in the
subject which is transformed.

The credit of having formulated this doctrine for the
first time belongs to Aristotle. He recognized that the real
is determined (against Heraclitus), but at the same time he
saw that it was determinable (against Parmenides). If the
real is *capable* of changing, the reason is that it possesses
within itself a real *power* of changing; a real *aptitude* to
become other; a real *principle* of determinability; in a word,
a real *potency*. Aristotle gave the name "act" to the realization of this potency, or the determination which is correlative to this determinability. Between *actual being* and
non-being, then, there is place for *potential* being; or more
exactly, being is divided into *actual being* and *potential being,*
into *act* and *potency.* This theory furnishes an explanation
for becoming, and permits us to avoid the extreme solutions
of Parmenides and Heraclitus. Every change is reduced
to the actualization of a potency, or to a passage from
potency to act.[1]

We are going to draw upon this Aristotelian doctrine in
our exposition of the first metaphysical law of change.

1. Aristotle never considered the hypotheses of "total realization" and
"annihilation."

Let us consider a subject *A*, which changes into *B*. Since the subject *A* was truly determinable *in itself,* we must state that it possesses a real potency for changing. This potency cannot be (1) the subject's *esse* (the principle of similarity), because the *esse* is the reason for perfect being, for opposition to non-being alone, for absolute determination and permanence. Nor can it be (2) the subject's *essentia* (principle of suchness), since the *essentia* is the reason for opposition to every other taleity, and consequently the reason for particular determination and permanence. In brief, the *esse* is the final reason for the subject's determination, while the *essentia* is the proximate reason. Hence the real potency for change which exists in the subject *A* must be a principle which is distinct both from the *esse* and the *essentia.*

We must look upon this real potency as a principle of being which is essentially correlative to the other principles constituting the subject. This new detail is implied in the data of the problem which we are trying to solve. For indeed it is the same subject *A* which *is,* which is *such,* and which *changes.* Change really affects the subject in itself. *I* walk, *I* reason, *I* grow, *I* die. If we stated that the potency for changing was a reality independent of the subject, then the change would affect this potency without affecting the subject itself. The power of changing, therefore, can only be a principle of being, essentially correlative to the other principles constituting the determinable subject. Consequently, this determinable subject (that is, the entire composite) is determined by reason of its principles of determination, *esse* and *essentia,* and determinable by reason of its principle of determinability.

This law which we have just formulated is still quite vague and indeterminate, and from the critical point of view it is not possible to make it more precise at present. We must look to experience to help us determine the exact nature of the real potencies explaining the different forms of change which we see in the world. Each particular type of change which we meet in experience implies a real potency of the same order.[2]

At this point we have to look once more at the question which we raised above: what is the relation between the doctrine of act and potency and the doctrine of the constitutive composition of the finite being?

Aristotle does not seem to have perceived the profound meaning and the metaphysical basis of his own theory of dynamism. If he had pushed his investigations further, he would have seen that change was a special case of multiplicity or diversity. He would have realized that he had first of all to solve the fundamental problem of pluralism, overcome monism, break out of the identical, and explain the diverse. The constitutive composition of the finite is the indispensable metaphysical basis for the doctrine of act and potency, because it is this composition which makes it possible for a perfect mode of being and an imperfect mode of being, and consequently act and potency, to be present in the real.

Can we use the terms "act" and "potency" to describe this constitutive composition? Is it exact to say that the existence is the *act* of the essence?

In the composite the *essentia* represents the imperfect mode of being; the *esse* represents the perfect mode of being. Consequently, it is by reason of its *essentia* that

2. In our development of general and special metaphysics, we shall show that there are two basic kinds of potencies: the potency of the substantial order or "prime matter," which in the case of corporeal beings is a component of the essence and the principle of substantial changes; and the potency of the accidental order or the "power of operation," which is the natural complement of the finite substance and the principle of accidental transformations.

the finite being is imperfect, and to that extent determinable, or "in potency" to become other. However, the *essentia* itself is not a "potency" in the strict sense, that is, a principle of determinability. It is not strictly a potency with respect to the *esse,* for the *essentia* is not a "perfectible" principle which would receive its perfection from the *esse.* The *esse* and the *essentia* are essentially correlative co-principles; they are absolutely inseparable; each one keeps its own nature in the composite. Nor is the *essentia* a potency or a principle of determinability with respect to some act different from the *esse,* since the *essentia* is a principle of taleity or determination and not a principle of change. In short, notwithstanding the usual way of speaking, we do not think that it is either exact or opportune to compare the composition of essence and existence to a composition of potency and act. To avoid all equivocation, it would seem better to restrict these notions of potency and act to the dynamic order, as Aristotle himself did.[3]

2. *The Relative Character of the Subject which Changes.* —Every change implies the intervention of a cause extrinsic to the subject which changes. In scholastic terms: *quidquid movetur, ab alio movetur.*

This new law states the extrinsic condition required for all becoming. As we have already noted, change as such is an abstraction. In the concrete or real order it is always *something* which changes; something appears, disappears, or evolves. In short, every change implies a *subject* which changes. The law which we have just formulated states that no subject can change by its own power without undergoing the influence of some extrinsic cause. We have stated above

3. We could show that the widening of the doctrine of potency and act, as carried out by the medieval Aristotelians and especially by St. Thomas, aimed at reconciling the Platonic metaphysics with that of Aristotle. It was an interesting and fruitful effort, but it did not entirely succeed.

what we mean by cause and by extrinsic cause. In the present instance, extrinsic cause is taken in the strict sense, that is, as an efficient cause.

Having cleared up these points we can now show that change cannot be understood only in terms of the subject affected. Change is a successive diversity, a successive "otherness"; "to change" (*moveri* in scholastic terminology) means to become other; it means to be successively A and then B. If we were to say that the passage from A to B was intelligible by itself, we would really contradict ourselves, for it would mean that we were at the same time affirming the fact of change (B is other than A) and denying it (A precontained B adequately; B, therefore, is not "other" than A); or we would identify being and non-being, because it would mean trying to explain being (the new determination B) by non-being (the absence of this determination in A).

We can sum up this line of argument in the following way:

Major: To change means to become other.

Minor: But if a thing adequately precontained the term of the change, it would not become other.

Conclusion: If the thing really changes, it does not adequately precontain the term of the change.

Change, therefore, is not intelligible as long as I restrict myself to the subject which changes. The principle of causality now obliges me to admit the existence of an extrinsic cause. We can put this new reflection in the following form:

Major: That which does not exist by itself (or that which is not intelligible by itself) exists by a cause (or is intelligible by a cause).

Minor: A subject which changes does not change (it
is not intelligible as changing) by itself.

Conclusion: A subject which changes does change (or
is intelligible as changing) by a cause.

We have introduced the principle of causality into the
proof of the metaphysical law expressing the extrinsic condition for all change. By stating more precisely what is
meant by the subject of the judgment "that which does not
exist by itself," we can now give more precise and less
general formulas for the principle of causality. In this
sense, the law stating the relativity of change can itself be
considered as a form of the principle of causality. "Every
subject which changes, depends on an extrinsic cause." More
exact study of the subject will give new formulas of the
principle of causality which will be even more restricted:
"That which begins to be, is caused"; "That which ceases to
be, is caused"; "That which is transformed, is moved by a
cause."

In order to show more clearly this relative character of
all change, we can apply the principle to the three possible
forms of change: (a) the change which is a total realization or passage from non-being to being: if we were to say
that this passage was explained by itself, then we would
make non-being the reason or the source of being; this, however, is meaningless; (b) the change which is total annihilation or passage from being to non-being: if we were to
say that this passage was explained by itself, then being
would be the reason or cause of non-being; but this is
absurd; (c) the change which is a transformation (a reality
which is, and which is such, becomes other; *A* becomes *B*):
if we were to say that this becoming was intelligible of itself,
then we would again confuse being and non-being, because

we make A the sufficient reason for B, that is, the sufficient reason for a determination which A did not possess; we would imagine then that A ceased to be itself, and became other by itself.

The principle stating the relativity of change has been frequently criticized by the defenders of absolute dynamism, and especially by Edouard Le Roy. We may sum up these criticisms in the form of the following objections and answer them briefly.

1. They say that the analysis of becoming involves a conceptual dissection of reality, and consequently the destruction of the concrete original becoming.

We reply: to say that state B of any subject is other than state A of the same subject, or to say that the oak is other than the acorn, or that the old man is other than the child, undoubtedly means that the focus of our attention is on two successive states of the same subject, but it does not contain any censurable dissection. It simply amounts to affirming the reality of the becoming, for if it were impossible or illicit to distinguish B from A, as these men claim, then there would be no becoming!

2. They further claim that to speak of "new determinations" means that we simply juxtapose these determinations to a pre-existing immobile subject. However, this would once again amount to destroying the spontaneity of the becoming; it would amount to denying life and destroying the expansion essential to the subject.

We reply: our view does not imply in any way the adding of completely formed extrinsic perfections. When we spoke about the law above, we saw that reality is far more complex than that. The "new determination" supposes a "determinability," a real power for changing; it is really the subject which changes and which evolves in itself. But we deny that this determinability suffices of itself to explain becoming, without the intervention of some cause extrinsic to the subject which changes.

3. Finally, these men charge that this metaphysical law which, it is claimed, *imposes itself a priori* on every change, is really an arbitrary law, a mere play of abstractions. They claim that we must get back to the real, we must observe life and the growth of the living organism, the progress of thought, and the will's activity. If we do that, they say, we will see everywhere the spontaneity of the *élan vital,* the unfolding of an inner dynamism, the development of the potencies of the being; but we will in no sense see passivity with regard to an extrinsic cause.

To tell the truth, it is rather strange to find this kind of difficulty advanced by an idealist like Le Roy for whom "anything beyond thought is unthinkable." Does he mean that thought would be exclusively dependent on sense intuition? Does he mean that thought could not formulate absolute metaphysical laws, valid for all possible experience? Whatever may be said about that point, experience in no way contradicts the metaphysical law which we have proposed, for if experience reveals everywhere the active spontaneity or dynamism of being (which our law in no way excludes), it just as clearly reveals the poverty of being and its dependence. The organism which develops depends constantly on its environment, and even the exercise of our spiritual activities depends on external factors. However, our reply would be incomplete if we did not add that it is metaphysical reflection which enables us to reach those basic relations of dependence which elude experience completely.[4]

4. On this point it would be well to read the critical study by Father J. Maréchal, "Le problème de Dieu d'après M. Edouard Le Roy," *Nouvelle Revue Théologique,* March-April, 1931.

Chapter III

DYNAMISM AS SHOWN IN THE ACTIVITY OF THE FINITE BEING

When we wish to make the metaphysical laws of becoming more specific, we find that we must appeal again to experience. Here our own lived experience of the changes occurring in the conscious self appears to have a privileged status. In fact, when we witness the changes taking place in the world of our objective experience, or in the bodies around us, we find it very difficult and often impossible to interpret these mysterious facts, because we see only the superficial manifestations of these changes, with the result that the exact nature of these changes almost invariably escapes us. Do these changes in bodies involve a simple "substitution" of one object for another? Or do they involve a "transformation"? Is this transformation profound or only superficial? Very often we cannot answer such questions. But when the change affects the self in its own conscious reality, the situation becomes much clearer: I am conscious of my own unity and independence; I am aware that I am the source or principle of certain changes taking place in me; and, finally, I am conscious that I keep my personal identity throughout the change which affects me. Privileged data of this kind allow me to undertake the metaphysical study of one of the most important kinds of change, that is, *activity*. They will help us develop a doctrine of activity which will be far more specific than our study of change in general.

Activity will appear to us as a property common to all finite beings. For this reason it belongs to general metaphysics.

§ 1. *Psychological Analysis of Activity as seen in Myself*

In epistemology we had already started to analyze activity considered as an immediate datum of consciousness.[1] But when we began to study the order of finite beings, we emphasized the characteristics which belong essentially to the self: unity and a certain dispersion, autonomy, and finiteness.[2] Combining these data, we now see that the self is a finite personal being, the principle of a certain inner evolution which really affects it but does not change its basic identity. This inner evolution is called *activity*.

Let us examine this mysterious fact a bit more closely, since we have this great advantage of being able to apprehend it in ourselves, in its inner reality and very source. The activity of the self manifests itself in the following way: In itself, it constitutes a change, a becoming, a novelty; it implies new determinations, new acts. These new acts belong to the self from a double point of view: (a) the self is in a certain way their principle; I am conscious that I am in some way the source of my acts; (b) the self is also the goal of these acts, since these acts exist for me, for my perfection, for my more complete development.

But these acts also have relations with the non-self. It is obvious that activity tends to put the self in contact with the non-self and to enrich the self through new contacts with surrounding realities.

Thus we see that activity is a very distinctive type of change. We can define it as follows: Activity is a change which comes from the finite being as its source. It does not alter the individuality of the finite being, but rather procures new perfection for it by relating it to other finite beings.

1. Van Steenberghen, *Epistemology,* pp. 99-107; 150-58.
2. See above, Part II, chap. I, § 1, n. 1-2.

In brief, activity shows that there is present in the finite being a certain mysterious power of expanding.

§ 2. *Metaphysical Interpretation of Activity*

The metaphysical laws of activity will try to connect activity with being and will try to explain activity as a modality of being. Since activity is a form of change, we will see that the laws which govern activity represent further precision and specification of the laws of change in general.

1. *Every Finite Being is Active.*—Every finite being is a principle of activity. The meaning of this first law is quite clear. It states that activity is an attribute of finite being as such; every finite being is not only perfectible, but is itself a spontaneous source of new perfection, a tendency to greater being, a capacity for acting. This thesis was stated frequently and used often by St. Thomas, but neither he nor his disciples ever proved it expressly.

We can find proof of this principle through a metaphysical analysis of the activity of the self. This sort of analysis of activity is privileged, since we can reach this activity by conscious reflection. This analysis shows us that in the finite being as such there is a necessary relation between existence and acting. We will try to show that the formal reason, or the necessary and sufficient reason, why I am a principle of activity is also found in every other finite being.

The formal reason why I am a principle of activity is that I *exist* in a *limited* way. Our psychological analysis of activity has already shown us that the self is, at least in some way, the principle of its activity. There is a certain causal relation between my being and my activity. It is clear that this fact of consciousness does not exclude the intervention of other factors extrinsic to the self. But here we are considering activity only in so far as it comes from the self.

We can make the relation existing between my being and my activity more precise by analyzing metaphysically the two terms of the relation. My being is a "certain kind of being" or finite being, that is, a composite formed by the union of a principle of perfection and a principle of measure. My activity means "more of a certain kind of being," that is, "increased being" which is itself finite, measured, and limited. I can adequately describe the concrete reality which I am in these terms: "a certain kind of being," "more of a certain kind of being."

But we can immediately give a more precise statement of the causal relation between my being and my activity. My capacity for more being cannot be explained by the limitation of my being. In other words, the principle by which I am limited and isolated cannot be the formal reason for my power of expansion. In the same way, the perfection of my being cannot be the reason for the limitation of my activity. The principle by which I am related to every being cannot be the formal reason for measuring my activity. Clearly, then, I must admit a twofold causal relationship. If I am capable of increased being, this can only be in virtue of my principle of perfection or my *esse*. This fact is not surprising because my *esse* is a principle of perfect being, by which I communicate with everything which exists. It is to be expected then that this principle would be the final reason for the dynamism manifested in me, that is, the active tendency which puts me in contact with the non-self. If my activity is limited, this can only be in virtue of my principle of limitation or my *essentia*. Again, this point can be seen without too much difficulty, for by limiting the perfection of the composite the *essentia* necessarily limits its powers of expansion.

In short, in the finite being which I am, existence as such is the formal reason for activity as such, and the suchness of existence is the formal reason for the suchness of activity. In other words, in me, "to be" means "to be a principle of activity," "to be such" means "to be the principle of a certain kind of activity." *Agere sequitur esse; agere sequitur formam.*

This formal reason why I am a principle of activity is common to all finite beings. We can state this second step in our proof as follows:

> *Major:* The fact that I exist in a limited way is the formal reason why I am a principle of limited activity.
>
> *Minor:* Every finite being possesses existence in a limited way.
>
> *Conclusion:* Every finite being possesses the formal reason why I am a principle of limited activity.

The major was proven in the first step of the reasoning. The minor is but the metaphysical definition of finite being.

An objection now naturally presents itself. Is the middle term of this syllogism, "to exist in a limited way," taken in the same sense in the two premises? This middle term includes two elements, "to exist" and "limited." It is readily granted that the term "to exist" keeps the same sense in the major and minor, since existence is the reason for the real likeness among finite beings. But the case is not at all the same for the second term, since the principle of limitation is precisely the principle of diversity for finite beings. It might seem, then, that this middle term is equivocal. From the fact that *my* principle of limitation does not exclude the power of acting, does it follow that *no* principle of limitation excludes it? Thus from the fact that *my* principle of limitation does not exclude the activity of knowing, does it follow that *no* principle of limitation excludes it, and that therefore every finite being is a principle of knowledge? Certainly not. The imperfection of the corporeal being excludes the activity of knowing. But then can we not conceive a finite being which would be so limited and isolated that its power of expansion would be completely arrested and suppressed?

The hidden fault of this objection is that it disregards the analogy of finite beings. Analogy cannot be broken down into a univocal element and an equivocal element. If finite beings were only existences they would coincide; they are analogous because they are *such existences;* that is, because they are all really *existences* but in different proportions to the measure of their *essence*. Their essence limits their participation in existence, but never destroys it. Consequently, they have in common not only *to exist,* but also to be *finite*. They all have a principle of taleity which limits the perfection of existence without destroying it. Hence the middle term in our syllogism is not equivocal in any way. It expresses a characteristic common to all finite beings.

The same answer can be given in a slightly different form. The objector grants that finite beings have the perfection of existence in common. Now in my case it is this perfection which is the formal reason for my active tending toward greater being. Hence every finite being, in so far as it exists, will possess this active tendency toward greater being. If such is the case, then to try to imagine an essence which would limit the existence to such an extent as to destroy its power of expansion really amounts to trying to imagine an essence which would limit the existence to the extent of destroying it, which is absurd.

Actually the example of knowledge merely confirms our argument. For in this case the objector appeals to a property which is not common to all finite beings. To be a principle of knowledge means to be the principle of a certain degree of activity, or of a certain level of activity. From our metaphysical analysis of activity we see that this level of activity involves a corresponding level of existence: *agere sequitur formam*. From the fact that I am a principle of knowledge, I can only conclude that those beings which possess the same degree of perfection as myself will also be principles of knowledge.

2. Composition of Substance and Power of Operation.— The activity of the finite being implies that there is present in the active subject a power of operation which is really distinct from the determining principles of the active subject.

This new principle is the application of the first law formulated above in the study of change in general. But the application here adds certain interesting details.

We have seen that every subject which changes possesses a real potency or principle of determinability in the order in which the change takes place, and that this principle is distinct from the *esse* and the *essentia*.

Now certain facts suggest that a change may affect a *subject in himself,* that is, in what constitutes him as a determined individual. In that case the change will alter the identity of the subject, and the subject will become *another* individual. A change of this kind must be explained by a real potency intrinsic to the essence itself; hence the essence must be considered to be composed of a principle of determination (form), and a principle of determinability (matter). Let us, for example, suppose it proven that the cat is an individual being, possessing its own *esse* and *essentia*. Let us also suppose it proven that the death of the cat is a change which affects it in its very identity, and that subsequently the cat's body is entirely reduced to matter; in brief, that the death of the cat is an "essential" or "substantial" change.[3] We would have to infer from this that the essence of the cat is not simple, but rather that it is composed of a principle of determination (the form, the soul) and a principle of determinability (matter). Metaphysical analysis of substantial transformations furnishes one of the traditional proofs of the hylomorphic composition. This, however, is really a problem for special metaphysics, because the composition of matter and form is not an attribute common to all finite beings.

Let us return to activity. Activity is certainly a transformation affecting the active subject. But it is not a radical or essential transformation. My activity has helped me to discover and describe the activity of every finite being, but this activity is a transformation which does not destroy my identity or personality, nor does it change my essence. Consequently, this activity should be explained not by some power intrinsic to the essence, but rather by a principle of determinability extrinsic to what properly constitutes the finite subject, that is, extrinsic to the composite of *esse* and *essentia*. For the future we shall call this complementary power of the finite being a *power of activity* or a *potency of operation*.

Thus, activity reveals another ontological aspect and a new metaphysical implication in finite being. Finite being is composed not only of *esse* and *essentia,* but this composite possesses *essentially,* by reason of its very nature, a complementary principle or power of operation which makes it capable of acting. To make the finite being intelligible as an

3. The precise meaning of this term will be determined later.

acting subject, we must say that it is composed of a subject and a power of operation.

We can determine the nature of this new composition to a limited extent.

In the first place, it is a question of a *duality of correlative principles,* or of essentially incomplete parts. If we took the composition to be merely a juxtaposition of autonomous realities, or even of independent parts, we would not explain what has to be explained—that is, how the one and the same concrete reality (the self, for example) can exist and act, perdure and become. The finite being perdures by reason of its principles of permanence, the *esse* and the *essentia;* it becomes by reason of its power of operation. The composite alone can be said to have full and real existence. The composite alone is the *complete principle of activity.* The composite alone is properly knowable; the two components are known only in an analogical and improper fashion in so far as they are metaphysical implications of the composite.[4] These components are, on the one hand, the finite subject constituted of *esse* and *essentia;* and on the other hand, the power of operation, which is the natural necessary complement of the subject, since activity is an essential attribute of every finite being.

In the second place, there is a *relation of subordination* between the power of operation and the subject. In this respect the composition for activity is quite different from the composition which constitutes the finite being. In this last

4. It should be noted that our knowledge of the ontological conditions of the finite being has developed gradually. We started from our knowledge of the concrete being as seized by a complete human intuition, and showed in succession the composition of *esse* and *essentia* and that of the subject and of the power of operation. *Esse, essentia,* subject, and power of operation represent, therefore, so many metaphysical inferences or implications, which we proved starting from the concrete being which alone is known in an immediate fashion.

composition the component principles belong to the same order, that of being or subsistence. By their union they co-operate to form the subsistent finite being. But in the composition for activity the relation of the component principles is quite different. This is no "proportion" between the subject and its power of operation. They belong to different orders. The *subject* is the reality which is principal, primary, constitutive of the individual, the reason for its permanence, the principle and goal of its activity. The power of operation is a complementary reality, secondary, subordinated, the principle of evolution of the individual, the principle of the "accidental" order, or the order of "secondary" perfection. It exists *by* the subject, *in* the subject, and *for* the subject. It makes the individual capable of acting.

Let us note here that properly speaking there is no potency-act relation between the subject and its power of operation. The subject is not determinable; it is in a sense already fully determined by its *esse*. The power of operation, then, is not properly speaking the act or determination of the subject. There is a potency-act relation between the power of operation and the operation itself—as, for example, between the intelligence and its act. The operation or activity is called the "second act" in opposition to the *esse* which is improperly called the "first act" of the being. The power of operation is called the "second potency" in opposition to the *essentia* which is improperly called the "first potency." [5]

This new composition which we have found is the *composition for activity*. It could be called an "operative composition," but this briefer expression is not exact, since this composition does not *make* the finite being act, but rather makes it *capable* of acting.

5. See above, Part II, chap. II, § 4, n. 1.

These component principles have been given different names. The principle of stability, or the subject, is called *substance (sub-stans); being in itself (ens in se); principal* or *first being; nature* (in the concrete sense, that is, substance in so far as it is determined or specified and the source of a certain activity). The principle of activity is called the *power of activity* or *operation (potentia operativa); inherent being (ens in alio;* as St. Thomas said: *proprie non est ens, sed entis); secondary or second* being; *accidental principle (accidit),* that is, the principle of the accidental order, of the order of second acts or secondary determinations of the finite being. The power of operation and the second acts make up this accidental order (the accidents) in opposition to the substantial order.

This composition for activity is a new metaphysical implication. It is an inference which must be made to explain the finite being which acts. Consequently, the component principles are not known in a proper fashion. Strictly speaking, we do not start from the accidents to prove the existence of the substance, nor vice versa. Rather we prove the composition by starting from the concrete composite which exists and acts.

This composition results from the constitutive composition and corrects it. It results from the constitutive composition because it is by reason of its taleity that the composite can acquire new determinations, and it is by reason of its existence that it shares in universal existence and implies a real similarity and imperfect identity with other beings.

Now we begin to see that this common possession of existence with all beings implies that the finite being has a real capacity for breaking out of its isolation; it implies a real power of expansion, an essential dynamism, a natural tendency to communicate with other beings. It also corrects the constitutive composition, for the constitutive composition solved the problem of the one and the many more in favor of the many. Consequently, the world of the finite tended to become *simpliciter diversum, secundum quid unum;* the finite composite was imprisoned in its own shell. However, the finite being's power of operation breaks this quarantine, makes the finite being capable of evolving and receiving further perfection and of being related to other finite beings.

3. *The Relative Character of the Active Subject.*—The activity of the finite being reveals dependence and a relation to an extrinsic cause. This principle is merely the application of the principle of relativity which we demonstrated when treating of change in general.

Major: Every subject which changes depends on an extrinsic cause.

Minor: The finite being which acts is a subject which changes.

Conclusion: The finite being which acts depends on an extrinsic cause.

What is this cause? We shall try to give more details later. For the present we shall content ourselves with noting the significance of this third principle. Even though the finite being may possess the power of acting, or the tendency to perfect itself of its very nature and in so far as it is, nevertheless it cannot be the adequate principle of its activity, for it cannot actuate or realize this power by itself. It cannot be the sole reason for the new perfection which it acquires by acting.

4. *Secondary Perfection.*—The finite being acquires its secondary perfection by means of activity. The meaning of

this final principle is quite evident. The activity, "increased being," or new perfection of which the finite being was the principle, constitutes the secondary perfection of that finite being. Existence or participation in existence constituted its first essential perfection. Activity is *for* the finite being, not the finite being for activity.

No further proof has to be given for this principle, since it follows immediately from the preceding ones. Activity proceeds *from* the finite being; it is the proper and proportionate act of the finite being's power of operation. By activity the finite being breaks out of its isolation, expands, realizes itself more fully, and in a certain way becomes "more than itself."

The theory of activity throws a good deal of light on the nature of the finite being and the mystery which it involves. This theory shows that the finite being is a principle of activity by means of an accidental power; but it is not the adequate principle of its own activity; and finally, it acquires its secondary perfection through activity, because by that it breaks out of its shell.

However, we have not yet listed everything which the status of a finite being involves. The most basic problem still remains. The solution of this problem will give us an entirely new outlook on the universal order of being.

CHAPTER IV

THE METAPHYSICAL ORDER

EVERY multitude which is reduced to unity, or every collection whose parts form a genuine whole, is called an *order*. Order is, then, the unity of many. The *static* order is the unity of a collection abstracting from changes which may affect it. The *dynamic* order refers to the unity of a collection whose elements are in motion; the implication is, therefore, that the movements affecting the various elements of the collection are correlated.

Our study of pluralism and dynamism disposed us to the idea that there was an order among finite beings. The universe as given to me in experience obviously presents a picture of extreme diversity. It is composed of many realities which are differentiated from each other, which oppose one another, and which are for that reason called "finite realities" or "finite beings." I myself am a finite being, surrounded by finite beings which I oppose, and which oppose one another. Pluralism holds that although these finite beings are distinct from each other, yet they are at the same time similar and are bound among themselves by a relation of similarity involving dependence or relativity. Dynamism holds that every finite being tries to break out of its isolation and enter into relation with other finite beings through activity; this however implies dependence, relativity, and the influence of a cause extrinsic to the acting subject. In brief, finite being reveals an essential and basic relativity in both its existence and activity. It is intimately connected with other finite beings. From such conclusions a new problem naturally arises; that is, does the collection of finite beings constitute a genuine order and, if so, how should we represent and explain such an order?

§ 1. The Order of Finite Beings

It is evident that the collection of finite beings constitutes a static order, since the very existence of these beings binds them together with a relation of adequate similarity. But do they also constitute a *dynamic order?* Do their various activities co-operate to bring about a harmonious evolution of the entire universe?

This is a far more complex problem and cannot be completely solved at the present time. It is true that we know that all finite beings have an essential *power* of expansion; they are all principles of activity, trying to break out of their isolation and establish relations with other beings. But can they all *really* act?

The finite being can act only in dependence on some extrinsic cause. What is this cause in the case of each finite being? Is it always present and always acting? None of the metaphysical principles formulated up to the present justifies any a priori statement that there is a perfect harmony existing among all finite beings, and that each one actually finds the complement which it needs for its power of acting in the order of finite beings. Can we show a dynamic order from our experience and observation of finite beings? Perhaps my experience can suggest some useful clues, but such experience is limited, and I have no grounds for believing that I know all the finite beings which exist or can exist. If such is the case, then an empirical investigation cannot help me discover the conditions common to all finite beings.

It is not easy to solve the problem even within the limited field of my own experience. This is so because of the difficulty of distinguishing individuals, a problem which in the field of inorganic matter seems insoluble at least for the present.[1] Let us suppose that it has been proved that my world of experience is composed of a multitude of finite individuals (myself, other men, animals, plants, the inorganic world). What do these finite individuals tell me about the existence of a dynamic order among them?

I myself am the source of a many-sided activity. Each element of my activity puts me in relation with the world about me. It is there that I find the necessary complements for my power of acting. I find things to know, to desire, to love, foods to assimilate, air to breathe, solid surfaces on which to sit, to lie, to move; I also find the temperature needed to conserve my life, and so forth. In return I furnish surrounding beings with the necessary complements for their power of acting. I can be the object of their knowledge and appetite (my dog seems to enjoy being petted, and so forth). Finally, the finite beings around me seem to behave in much the same way toward each other; each one gives and receives; each one lives from its environment and for its environment.

However, things do not run along absolutely smoothly. Men and animals sometimes die of hunger, thirst, suffocation or cold. In other words, these beings fail to find in their environment the complement which they need for their power of acting. Other living beings may perish by fire or water; still others from the effect of some poison, some weapon, or some violent blow. Such beings found elements around them which positively opposed their power of acting. We see also that there are beings which are completely

1. See above, Part II, chap. 1, § 1.

absorbed by others; thus a cabbage is eaten by a rabbit, and the rabbit in turn is eaten by a fox. This sort of thing would seem to suggest that there is a "disorder" in nature, and a lack of harmony among beings. It may be that these facts reveal laws which are more complex than the simple laws of harmonious adaptation among activities; perhaps they show laws of subordination of inferior beings to superior beings, of individuals to the common good of the universe, and so forth.

To sum up, our world of experience shows us that there exists a *certain* dynamic order in the corporeal world; it shows that various exchanges take place among the finite beings which make it up; that there are mutual beneficial influences among the active subjects; that in a great number of cases the active subjects do get the complement which they need for their power of acting. There is a certain pre-established harmony among beings, there is a mutual finality, a disposition to perfect one another. But this order does not seem to be absolute, for certain beings do not find the complement which their power of acting needs, while the influence of the environment is positively harmful to others, so much so that they are sometimes completely eliminated in the struggle for survival.

We asked earlier whether the collection of finite beings formed an "order." For the present our answer must be that finite beings do form a static order; the beings of which we have distinct knowledge seem to form a certain dynamic order. This, however, does not seem to exclude all disorder; we do not know whether finite beings exist outside the world of our experience, nor do we know the conditions in which they might act.

But is this more or less perfect order of finite beings sufficient for itself? Can it be identified with the sum total of reality? In that hypothesis what would be the absolute or unconditioned reality, whose existence obtruded upon us from the very start of ontology? [2] Would this absolute be the order of finite beings as such? Or would it be only a part of this order (as, for example, the world of spirits)? Would it be some finite being superior to all the rest, on which all the rest would depend? These are new problems, arising naturally at this point, which concern the order of finite beings.

The investigations made above have already suggested an answer, since they have shown us that the finite being taken by itself has only a relative character. All that we have to do now in order to reach a complete and fully satisfying solution to this problem, is to continue those reflections and develop them more fully.

§ 2. The Transcendent Principle of the Order of Finite Beings

In general, philosophers do not find it hard to admit the relativity of the finite being taken separately, at least when it is a question of the finite beings given in the world of our human experience, for everything about them shows that they are bound up with others and that they belong to an order. Their ontological similarity shows their relationship with all beings; their activity puts them in relation with their environment; and even the deficiencies or disorders which sometimes mark their activity, far from contradicting their basic relativity, merely stress more emphatically the indigence of the finite being, dependent as it is on the environment in which it acts.

But some philosophers are inclined to say that the collec-

2. See above, Part I, chap. I, § 4, n. 3.

tion of finite beings, or the order of finite beings, constitutes the sum total of all reality and provides the final explanation of all things. To complete our metaphysical study of finite beings, therefore, we must show that this view is absolutely insufficient and entirely unacceptable.

1. *A Finite Being is Totally Relative.*—Every finite being is a totally relative and conditioned being. The total dependence of the finite being is revealed both in its existence and in its activity.

(a) *In its existence.* In our treatment of pluralism we showed that every finite being is a caused being.[3] This is so because the fundamental kinship which every finite being has to other beings can be understood only after we see that it is the consequence of a relation of *total* dependence; in other words, when we see that the finite being is conditioned in its very *existence*.

(b) *In its activity.* Our study has shown us that activity implies dependence on an extrinsic cause. We must now show that this dependence is not merely the more or less superficial dependence involved when bodies act on one another, but rather that it is a basic and radical dependence in existence.

Finite being is a principle of activity by reason of its very existence. Its power of operation is essential to it. The nature and extent of its activity will result from its substantial nature or quiddity. Now all this implies a complete relativity from every point of view.

The determinability or *perfectibility* of the active being furnishes a first sign of its relativity, for an absolute being cannot be perfectible, since perfectibility implies the capacity of being influenced by a cause. Now the perfectibility of

3. See above, Part II, chap. I, § 4, n. 3.

the finite being is due to its very *essence,* its principle of limitation. The relativity of the finite being is therefore *essential* to it, affecting the very constitutive principles of the finite being.

The active tendency or *power of expansion* of the finite being is a second indication of relativity, since the goal of this tendency is the perfecting of the finite being by making it break out of its isolation, and by developing it through union with other finite beings. The finite being has this power by reason of its *esse.* Here again then, relativity is basic, since it affects even the constitutive principles of the finite being.

The need which the active being shows of finding a *complement for its power of acting* in other beings, is the result of the isolation in which its essence encloses it. Consequently, it is the result of an essential limitation. This provides a new basic sign of relativity.

Every time activity actually takes place it reveals a *pre-established harmony.* This is not a merely superficial harmony, but a harmony among *natures,* among active substances, which consequently are fundamentally orientated to one another and capable of mutually developing one another by their activities.

Once the finite being has acquired the complement needed for its power of acting, it possesses an active power of producing its secondary act, of really being the principle of that act and, to that extent, of going beyond itself. This active power shows that the finite being is subject in its very existence to a cause which gives it this power of expansion, or of surpassing itself, by the very fact of making it exist.

We can see, then, that the activity of the finite being reveals a basic relativity and a radical dependence from every point of view. Even in its constitutive reality, the finite being is relative to something other than itself. Here, once again, we see that an "absolute finite being" is a contradiction in terms, for in so far as it was a finite being, it would include the power of acting, while in so far as it was an absolute being, it must exclude that power.

2. *The Order of Finite Beings is Totally Relative.*—The order of finite beings is totally relative or conditioned. We have seen that every finite being considered separately is relative or conditioned in its very existence. But it might be claimed that the finite being was merely relative to other finite beings, that it depended on the whole order of finite beings, and that this order as a whole was the absolute or unconditioned reality.

This latest effort to explain the finite only by the finite is entirely illusory, and it belongs to imagination rather than to thought. In fact, the order of finite beings is merely the collection of finite beings, and if each of them is conditioned in its very existence, then the order of finite beings will not include any unconditioned reality and will not, therefore, contain the ultimate explanation of the real. It is true that we can get a new total effect by adding several elements together, provided that each of these elements has its own reality and power. Thus a number of stones can form an arch because each of them contributes its own reality, geometrical form, and weight to the construction. Several horses can co-operate to pull a wagon because each of them contributes its own muscular force to the total effect. But though we can multiply totally relative beings as much as we like, we will never get an absolute being from it, any more than we could move a carriage by harnessing to it animals whose individual moving force was nil.

This basic deficiency of the order of finite beings can be

brought out still more explicitly by examining the problem first on the level of existence, then on the level of activity.

(a) *On the level of existence.* The collection of finite beings cannot explain the ontological similarity which unites all these separate beings in the order of existence (or the static order), just as no one of the finite objects themselves can explain that similarity to others. Since, indeed, all of them are finite, that is, opposed to each other, strangers to each other, separate from each other, no one of them can contain the other as its total cause, and consequently the ontological similarity among them remains unexplained.

(b) *On the level of activity.* This radical indigence is also shown on the level of activity or in the dynamic order, for the real expansion of finite beings through activity could not be explained by the collection of them. Activity cannot in fact be reduced in any sense to mere receptivity. To act is not merely "to receive" a second act; it is to "produce" that act, to be the principle of that act. If the active being has to receive a certain complement to its power of activity from the beings surrounding it, this is only a preliminary condition for its own activity. It is a condition whose function is to relate the active subject to its environment and direct its activity in a certain sense. But the secondary act itself is an "increase of being." The true principle of that act is the finite being in so far as it is. The act is a *new perfection* having its immediate source in the active substance itself, which is set off from all other finite substances by its constitution as a finite being. This being the case, it is evident that we cannot take the activities of the finite being to be mere "exchanges" among finite beings, exchanges which would not affect the global perfection of the entire order of finite beings at all. On the contrary, since each of the active substances comprising that order is a source of new perfections, the *whole order of finite beings is perfected,* enriched, and developed. The whole order receives an increase of perfection, thanks to the activity of the finite beings. In a word, the order of finite beings is perfectible. Now an absolute being cannot be perfectible, because every change implies dependence on an extrinsic cause. Consequently, the order of finite beings is not an absolute reality.

We have just expressed an important corollary of the law of relativity of change: *the sum total of reality as such is immutable.* We have already seen that the sum total of reality as such, the totality outside which there is nothing, cannot be conditioned by anything else, for there is nothing outside of it. As a whole, it exists by itself; it is of itself everything which it is.[4] Here a new characteristic of the sum total as such forces itself on us, that is, its immutability.

This will be clear from the following syllogism:

Major: Every change implies a cause which is extrinsic to the subject which changes.

Minor: Now, the sum total of reality as such cannot depend on any extrinsic cause.

Conclusion: Therefore, the sum total of reality as such excludes all change and all possibility of change.

As a consequence it is absurd to suppose that the totality of that which exists had a beginning, or that this totality will one day cease to exist, or that it might as a whole become other. Change can be conceived only as a modification within the universe, as an alteration which affects this or that element without affecting the whole as such.

3. *The Existence of the Infinite Being.*—The order of finite beings is completely conditioned by the infinite being.

4. See above, Part I, chap. I, § 4, n. 3.

We now possess all the elements required to solve the problem of the absolute. A final metaphysical inference will enable us to discover the supreme ontological implication of reality and, at the same time, to reach the highest point of human thought which is the culminating point of metaphysics. The radical opposition which we see between the finite and the absolute logically compels us to the affirmation of a being which transcends the order of finite beings, beings which are composed, perfectible, and relative. We are driven logically to the affirmation of a being which is not finite, but "infinite."

This discovery would be exciting for the man who would actually live it, who would see directly into all its moral and religious implications. But for most of us it has only a theoretic or scientific interest, because the existence of the Infinite Being has become in our eyes almost a commonplace. Furthermore, even though this supreme step of metaphysical reflection gives us a reality which is new for us, further reflection is needed to bring out the attributes of the Infinite Being and to arrive at a knowledge of the personal and provident God, whose discovery can completely transform our picture of the world and life.

The *metaphysical inference* which reveals the existence of the Infinite Being to us, is very simple. An absolute reality forces itself upon us; we cannot find this absolute reality in the order of finite beings; consequently, it must transcend the order of finite beings and is, therefore, non-finite or infinite. In this way we pass from *proper* but *confused* knowledge of the unconditioned being to the *improper* or *analogical* but distinct knowledge of the Infinite Being, by means of the proper and distinct knowledge which we have of the essentially relative finite being.

This process of thought can be expressed in the following logical schema:

Major: That which exists is either finite or non-finite (by reason of the principle of the excluded middle).

Minor: An absolute reality does exist.

Conclusion: Therefore, the absolute reality must be either finite or non-finite.

Minor: But this reality is not finite (because everything finite is relative).

Conclusion: Therefore, this reality must be non-finite or infinite.

It is evident that our spontaneous thinking lacks the precision and method shown in this logical schema. To put a reasoning process into form always calls for a reflective, artificial effort. But an effort of this sort does serve to bring out better the connections which are unexpressed in spontaneous thought, and checks the accuracy of its conclusions.

The reasoning which we have just analyzed tries to make the nature of the absolute more precise by means of a disjunctive syllogism which expresses the alternative of the finite and the infinite. A parallel line of reasoning enables us to bring out the *relation of causality* which binds the finite to the infinite. This time the proof is based upon the alternative of the absolute and the relative, that is, of the unconditioned and the conditioned; and it concludes that the order of finite beings exists in complete dependence on the Infinite Being. The proof in form is as follows:

Major: That which exists is either absolute or it is relative to the absolute.

Minor: The order of finite beings does exist.

Conclusion: Therefore, it is either absolute or it is relative to the absolute.

Minor: But it is not absolute.

Conclusion: Therefore, it is relative to the absolute, that is (by reason of the preceding conclusion), to the Infinite.

The metaphysical study of finite beings ends, therefore, in the recognition of an Infinite Being which is the adequate cause of the order of finite beings. In other words, this study is completed by the metaphysical proof of the existence of God, for we will show shortly that the Infinite Being possess all the attributes which characterize the divinity in our eyes. It is well worth our while then to examine attentively this final metaphysical inference which forms the proof for the existence of God, to bring out its salient points more strongly.

The proof of the existence of the Infinite Being is an a posteriori not an a priori proof. A proof can be called a priori in two different senses. The proof may be one which has its starting point in an idea or principle of the ideal order; such was the ontological proof of St. Anselm, which in the usual interpretation started from the idea of the most perfect possible being. Or the proof may be one which establishes the effect starting from the cause; thus, the astronomer shows that there will be an eclipse of the sun at a certain time and bases his view on the causes of this phenomenon (the movements of the sun, of the earth, of the moon). The a posteriori proof, on the other hand, is either one which starts from a datum of experience, or one which proceeds from effect to cause. Our proof of the existence of the Infinite Being is an a posteriori proof in both senses of the term. It is based upon an affirmation of existence (something exists, finite beings exist) and not upon an idea or a principle; secondly, it goes from effects (finite beings) to the cause (the Infinite Being). It does not try to deduce the existence of effects from the existence of a cause.

The proof of the existence of the Infinite Being is a metaphysical proof and not one which belongs to the empirical order. The Infinite Being is not an object of experience, nor an object of immediate perception. We cannot discover it as we might discover some new or hidden phenomenon by means of more sensitive and more highly developed scientific instruments, for the Infinite Being does not belong in any way to the world of our human experience or to the world of our proper knowledge. We must prove that He exists. We can reach Him only as a metaphysical implication of experience, as the condition for the intelligibility and possibility of experience. The proof of the existence of the Infinite Being necessarily requires a metaphysical reflection, that is, a reflection bearing upon being as such and upon the conditions of the real as such. We must re-think the experience from which we start in terms of its metaphysical value. Only a genuine metaphysical reflection can enable us to go beyond the order of experience as such and affirm that something *must* be, that *every* finite being, even those outside the world of human experience, is relative or conditioned.

This affirmation of the Infinite Being is, therefore, the natural and necessary culmination of metaphysical research. This affirmation will shed new light upon all the preceding steps, and will solve all the difficulties thus far unresolved.

The metaphysical nature of the proof for the existence of God gives it an absolute validity and a critical value which is surpassed only by the direct evidence of an object grasped immediately in itself without any recourse to discursive reasoning. Consequently, like all the theses of ontology, this affirmation of the Infinite Being gives to every open mind capable of understanding the value of the proof a supreme degree of certitude (metaphysical certitude, proper to absolutely necessary truth). But the human mind is never completely open to metaphysical truths; it feels a sort of dizziness when it has to pass beyond the field of experience or of its own proper knowledge and venture into the obscure regions of metaphysical inference. Furthermore, it does not too willingly submit to the asceticism of reason and abstract reflection, where sensibility is no longer gratified. This explains the psychological uneasiness and feeling of unrest which may remain in many minds even on the conclusion of the most rigorous metaphysical demonstrations. But the true friends of wisdom, those who wish to "adore in spirit and in truth," try to guard against these unjustified impressions, which often reveal the influence of an unsuspected empiricist bent of mind.

The proof of the existence of the Infinite Being is really one, but this unity involves a certain duality. The affirmation of the Infinite Being involves three elements: (1) knowledge that an absolute is necessary; (2) knowledge that the finite as such is relative; (3) a realization of the opposition between absolute and the finite. Now it is clear that the whole force of the proof rests on our proving that the finite as such is relative. It is at this point that a certain duality enters into the demonstration, because we can show that the finite is relative either on the level of existence or on the level of activity. These two ways are independent of each other, but an understanding of one helps to an understanding of the other. In addition, they share a common starting point in the metaphysical interpretation of the finite being, because to know that *every* finite being is perfectible by activity, we must know the metaphysical nature of the finite being and its constitutive composition. Consequently, the proof from activity that the finite being is relative is not completely autonomous.

Finally, let us note that our formulation of the proof of the existence of the Infinite Being seems to be the *only rigorous proof that can be given to show the existence of God*. In other words, we believe that this metaphysical proof is unique or exclusive; we believe that every really satisfactory proof must be reducible to it. The term "God" is, indeed, ordinarily taken to designate the Creator of the universe, that is, the first unique Cause of everything which exists. Any nominal definition which did not express that point would be insufficient because it would not indicate the true God, the first principle and last end of all things, especially of man. Now in order to show the existence of this first unique Cause, we must go beyond the finite *as such,* we must show the relativity of the finite *as such,* and this can only be done by a critical metaphysical evaluation of its existence and its activity.

If this is the case, what can be said about the innumerable proofs that have been proposed in the course of time?

It seems impossible to reduce their extreme variety to one single metaphysical proof. Must we then completely reject this great effort which human thought has made in its search for God?

Certainly not. But there is great need for more precision and discernment. Let us note a few essential points.

We must first winnow the wheat from the chaff. Many proposed proofs were bungled and evidently cannot be accepted. Such were the attempts at scientific, physical, biological, geological, and even mathematical proofs, of the existence of God. Also the proof of St. Anselm, at least as it is usually understood.

Secondly, many so-called arguments for the existence of God are really only psychological preparations and not properly proofs at all, though they may prepare the mind to seek and find God. Under this heading may be listed (1) arguments from authority: from the universal consent of peoples, the agreement of great thinkers, the testimony of great mystics. (2) Arguments which create presumptions in favor of the existence of God: the argument that without God the moral and social order would not have a solid basis. (But does this order impose itself on us? Might it not proceed from an agreement—at least implicit—which men realized they had to make if they were to live together?) (3) Arguments which are simply an invitation to further reflection: the arguments based on the marvels which nature shows in all its domains; cases of miracles; examples of heroic sanctity; facts of the mystical order; in brief, every datum of experience which apparently reveals a superhuman wisdom, power or providence. Facts of this kind can stimulate our search for God, but they must be developed by further metaphysical reflection if they are to provide us with a distinct and certain knowledge of the Creator. (4) Arguments which are really preludes to the metaphysical proof: those studies which strive to emphasize some particular manifestation of contingency in the finite being such as the deficiencies of material beings, the mortality of man, the solidarity of natures in the corporeal world, and so forth. Considerations of this kind can provide useful introductions to the more general problem of the relativity of the finite being as such. (5) Arguments, finally, which should be considered rather *approximations* of the metaphysical proof. Such arguments contain elements which form an intrinsic part of the metaphysical proof, but in themselves they are incomplete or imperfectly presented. Sometimes they do show the necessity of an absolute, but they do not make its nature precise. Sometimes they restrict themselves to showing the contingency of a certain class of finite beings; for example, corporeal beings. Sometimes they try to prove the relativity of the finite being as such, but they do not completely succeed. Sometimes, too, all the essential elements of the proof are present, but they are badly arranged or imperfectly expressed.

The *quinque viae* of St. Thomas are among the most interesting approximations of the genuine metaphysical proof. They are representative arguments which merit examination. The more so, since they enjoy an extraordinary prestige among scholastics and are often reproduced rather indiscriminately out of their true context, and without the necessary explanations.[5]

The *prima via* is drawn from Aristotle and amounts to this: there is movement and becoming in the world; now that which changes is under the influence of a cause which moves it; and since we cannot ascend indefinitely in the series of *moved movers,* we must finally stop at an *unmoved mover,* that is, at a first mover which is God. The reasoning as such is well defined and accurate, but it does not permit us to conclude immediately to the unicity of the First Principle. From the fact that every changeable being is dependent, it follows that there exists at least one unchangeable Being at the origin of all the changes taking place in the universe. But how can we show that there exists only one such being? Aristotle proved the unicity of the First Mover on astronomical grounds derived from the unity of the cosmos and the unicity of the first changeable or the first

5. *Summa Theologica,* I*, qu. 2, art. 3.

heaven. St. Thomas pursued this same line of thought in the first part of the *Summa Contra Gentiles* (I, cap. 13). In the *Summa Theologica* the points derived from the Aristotelian astronomy have happily been left aside, but the proof of the unicity of the First Mover is also lost with them. Thomas was well aware of this fact since he proposed a proof of the divine unicity in Question XI. If we wish the *prima via* to lead to an explicit affirmation of the one true God, we must be prepared to make use of Thomas' development up to that point. This added deduction will consist in showing that all finite beings are changeable and that consequently only the infinite and unique Being can be the unchangeable mover or First Mover.

The *secunda via* is also inspired by Aristotle. It can be summarized as follows: there is in the universe a hierarchy of causes and effects; now this hierarchy cannot be reduced to a series, even an infinite series, of caused causes, that is, of effects; for unless there is a first cause which is not caused, the whole series becomes impossible. We must then rise to an uncaused first cause which is God. Here again the reasoning involved causes no difficulty provided that the existence of a hierarchy of causes was properly established at the point of departure. But this reasoning of itself proves only that the absolute (the need of which is again supposed) should be sought for beyond all dependent causes and that therefore there exists one or several first causes. This proof also requires a complement, and St. Thomas later on spares no efforts to show that every finite being is a caused being.

The *tertia via* was doubtless inspired by Moses Maimonides, but it has been recently proved that its true source is to be found in Aristotle.[6] In the *Summa Theologica* the

6. H. Holstein, "L'origine aristotélicienne de la 'tertia via' de Saint Thomas," *Revue philosophique de Louvain*, August, 1950, pp. 354-70.

form of the proof is complicated and questionable, due perhaps to an excessive fidelity to the ideas of the Philosopher.
The formulation found in the *Summa Contra Gentiles* (I,
cap. 15) is much more satisfactory. As expressed there, the
reasoning amounts to this: there exist beings which are
contingent; now every contingent being is caused; consequently the contingent can be explained only by the necessary. But the necessary in turn can be either necessary of
itself, or it can draw its necessity from a cause. In this
latter case we must rise to a being which is necessary of
itself. In any hypothesis, then, we will arrive at a being
necessary of itself, which is God. This argument proves only
that *there exists one or several absolute beings* (necessary of
themselves), and that we must look for the absolute beyond
the contingent realities of this world. Once again, the proof
is incomplete and requires further development.

The *quarta via* is fashioned from Aristotelian elements,
but it has a definitely Neo-platonic complexion. In the
Summa Theologica it is stated as follows: things are more
or less good, true, noble, and so forth; now the term "more
or less" implies a maximum; therefore, there must exist a
maximum of goodness, truth, nobility, and consequently of
being. And since the maximum in a given order is the cause
of all the inferiors in that order, there must exist a supreme
being which is the cause of the being, goodness, truth and
nobility of all other things, and this being is called God. In
this instance the proof is developed entirely on the metaphysical level and it concludes directly to the existence of the
unique creative Cause. But the proof still leaves itself open
to serious criticism. The principle that "the more and less
are so called with respect to a maximum" is certainly not
true in all cases, for "the more and less" are often so designated with respect to a unit of measure. Thus a person is

more or less rich according as he possesses a more or less impressive number of "francs" or "dollars." The more and less hot are so named with respect to the unit of heat which is the degree of a thermometer, and not with respect to a *maxime callidum,* as Thomas claimed on the basis of a physics which is today outmoded. If we restrict the principle to the transcendental values, then it is true but not immediately evident. It becomes evident only after we have proven that the *Maximum Reale* exists, in other words, when the proof of the existence of God has been completed.

Nor is it true without qualification that the greatest in any order is always the cause of its inferiors. The richest man is not the cause of the riches of others. Consequently, we must determine the precise conditions in which the principle is true. In brief, the *quarta via* as expressed in the *Summa Theologica* fails to prove that there exists at the summit of the hierarchy of beings an absolute Maximum (the Infinite Being) and not merely a relative Maximum (the most perfect of finite beings). St. Thomas gives a much better expression to the argument elsewhere, as for example in *De Potentia,* III, 5. The formula given there can be stated in the following reasoning: finite beings, while opposing one another as finite beings, are basically similar by their being, their unity, their truth, their goodness. Now the fact that beings which are diverse and opposed are nevertheless similar, reveals that they have a common dependence on a Being which precontains them as Cause and which consequently is not finite. Consequently, there exists at the origin of all finite beings a non-finite or Infinite Being, which is the fullness of being *(Maximum Ens)* in which all the others participate according to the degree of their essence *(magis et minus)*. Thus we see that the corrected restatement of the *quarta via* coincides with the metaphysical proof which was proposed above.

The *quinta via* also develops Aristotelian concepts. The argument reminds us of the views of St. John of Damascus and Averroës, but St. Thomas gives a new twist to it in the *Summa Theologica.* He says certain things which lack knowledge tend to realize an end. This implies guidance by an intelligent cause, just as the direction of the arrow toward a determined target implies the intervention of an archer. Consequently, there exists an intelligence or a providence ordering natural beings to their end, and this we call God. The comparison with the arrow is misleading and should be discarded. The arrow by nature has no movement or determined direction, and if it follows a definite direction this can only be under the influence of an extrinsic cause. If this direction reveals an intention, it also indicates at the same time an intelligent cause. But the beings of which St. Thomas is here speaking have a *nature* which is the principle of a determined activity. They can act only according to that nature. Consequently, it is not surprising that they act in a definite way. We must, therefore, stress the fact that a finite nature which gives rise to a finalised tendency reveals the intervention of an intelligence. If this nature is not intelligent itself it proves the existence of an Intelligence capable of creating it. But we would still have to show that all finite natures proceed from the same creative Intelligence, which would amount to showing that these natures are conditioned beings. We can show this by analyzing the active tendency manifested by these natures, and by the basic relativity implied in this tendency. But such a line of development clearly brings us back to the metaphysical proof which we proposed above.

Very important conclusions flow from this brief survey

of the *quinque viae*. In Question II and the following
questions of the *Summa Theologica* we can find all the elements required to elaborate the metaphysical proof of the
existence of God. But these elements are scattered and are
often mixed with other elements which are rather questionable or quite unacceptable. No one of the five ways is sufficient by itself. No one of the five ways can be presented as
it stands, as a complete rigorous proof of the existence of
God. The first two have to be developed with the help of
the later questions of the *Summa*. The other three need to
be corrected and completed. In any case, if we separate the
quinque viae from their general context, and especially if
we separate them from subsequent questions of the *Summa
Theologica,* we mutilate the work in a way which is both
dangerous and unjustified. We should not be surprised at
the imperfections which we have uncovered in the statement
of the *quinque viae*. They are the unavoidable consequences
of the historical environment in which St. Thomas lived and
worked. Every thinker must of necessity express his
thought in the language of his own period and in function of
the state of knowledge of his own time. If by some impossible chance he did not do this, his contemporaries would
find him unintelligible. Our task should be to present the
teaching of the Common Doctor in such a way as to take
cognizance of the progress made in philosophical thought
and the legitimate needs of the present day. Otherwise we
run the risk of compromising the permanent value and spread
of his profound thought.[7]

Can we express the proof of the existence of God in more
popular terms?

It is only natural that many people should raise such a

7. Van Steenberghen, "Reflexions sur les 'quinque viae,'" *Acts of the
Third International Thomistic Congress* (Rome, 1950).

question. For the problem of God is not merely a problem of philosophy, it is also a problem of absorbing human interest. The problem is how can we express the proof of the existence of God in a way that would be understandable to the average man.

We can sum up our reply as follows: the broad field of "psychological preparations" [8] can and should be expressed in popular form. But we ought to present these arguments honestly for what they are and for what they are worth. The strict metaphysical proof can be popularized only to the extent to which metaphysics itself can be popularized.

In this matter we have to avoid exaggerating the difficulty of this type of reflection, or of underestimating its difficulty. While it is quite evident that many men are not in a frame of mind even to understand the statement of a metaphysical problem, yet it is also certain that every man is an unconscious metaphysician and will at times give flashes of metaphysical insight. By definition every intelligent being is capable of thinking about being and is curious to understand that which exists.

We must wake this dormant metaphysical ability, we must stimulate this blunted curiosity and excite the love of truth in man. We must remind man of the incomparable nobility of his power of thought, and stimulate him into making the effort needed to grasp at least the essential steps of man's intellectual ascent to the Infinite. For God has given us an intellect primarily that we may seek after Him.[9]

8. See above, Part II, chap. IV, § 2, n. 3.
9. Some further notes on the problem of God will be found in three articles by the author under the general title "Le problème philosophique de l'existence de Dieu," *Revue philosophique de Louvain,* Feb., May-August, Nov., 1947, pp. 5-20; 141-68; 301-13.

§ 3. Conclusion: Finite Being and the Attributes of Being

At the close of our metaphysical study of finite being we can look into a final question which will allow us to sum up the results of all our previous investigations. It will also give us a broader understanding of the ontological laws governing the finite being. *How do being and its transcendental attributes belong to finite being?* We know that these attributes are analogous just as being itself is, and that they belong to every being according to its own proper nature.

The finite being is being but not fully, since it is *finite*. The tension within it, between its being and its finiteness, is revealed in its tendency to action. Since it is entirely caused by the Infinite Being, and since it is a "participation" of His unlimited being, finite being necessarily tends to go beyond its own strict limits and to communicate with everything which is, as far as its essence or nature will permit it.

The finite being is *distinct* not only from non-being or from that which is not, but also from everything which it is not. It is distinct from other finite beings by *opposition;* it is *aliquid,* that is, *aliud quid.* It immediately becomes determinable, and a certain communion or even a certain confusion can be had between it and other finite beings. It is distinct from the Infinite Being by *participation,* but it is entirely *relative* to its Cause.

The finite being is *undivided,* but not perfectly, since it is composed, in the order of subsistence and in the order of activity.

The finite being is *similar,* but with reservations, for it is at the same time dissimilar, different, and alien with respect to every other finite being. The ontological similarity of the finite to its Infinite Cause does not exclude the absolute transcendence of the Infinite with respect to the finite being.

The finite being is *intelligible,* but it is not fully intelligible by itself; it is fully intelligible only in the order of finite beings and in subordination to the Infinite Being.

Lastly, the finite being is *desirable,* but since it is not fully intelligible by itself, neither can it fully satisfy the intellectual appetite or the will by itself alone.

The derivation of the attributes of the Infinite Being will enable us shortly to bring out still better the contrast between the way in which the transcendental properties belong to the finite and the way in which they belong to the Infinite.

Part Three

INFINITE BEING

FOR us the Infinite Being is a "metaphysical implication" in the same sense as are the constitutive composition of the finite being and its compositions in the dynamic order. When speaking of these first metaphysical implications, we said that we would have to depend on the method of inference which discovered these realities, if we wished to learn anything further about their nature. In other words, we can only make more explicit what is already contained in the conclusion of the inference. The same point holds for the Infinite Being. We can know its nature and attributes only in so far as these attributes are implied in the proof of its existence.

Once we grasp this fact, we will see that the philosophical study of God *does not constitute a science which would be distinct from ontology*. According to the strict principles of rational systematization, we should have described the derivation of the attributes of God at the end of the preceding chapter as a simple corollary to the proof of His existence. If we devote a distinct section to this study, it is only because of its considerable length.

For this reason we cannot follow the views of those authors who since the nineteenth century have tried to set up the philosophical study of God as a distinct discipline, which is sometimes called "natural theology," sometimes "theodicy," [1] sometimes "special metaphysics." It had al-

---

1. The term "theodicy" comes from Leibniz and means "a defense of God." Two objections can be raised to its use: first, the science has nothing in common with rhetoric; secondly, God has no need of a "defense."

ready been observed in the Middle Ages that God is not a *subjectum scientiae* in philosophy, that is, an object of study which could form the basis and starting point for an independent scientific discipline. For the philosopher, God forms the object of a *conclusion* to general metaphysics.

It may now be asked what can be known about the Infinite Being except that He exists? St. Thomas himself says, *"de Deo scimus quia est, sed non quid sit."* Have not the greatest thinkers of history stressed strongly the inaccessible, impenetrable, and unknowable character of the Infinite Being? Must we not admit that our human concepts are completely inadequate to cope with the mystery of God? In short, do not both wisdom and a proper respect for the divine transcendency dictate an attitude of agnosticism?

When, however, we reflect on the formula used by St. Thomas, we get the impression that it must be somewhat over-simplified. For how can I know that a thing exists without getting some sort of knowledge of what it is, that is, without knowing whose existence or what existence it is that I know? How can the term "God" have any sense at all for me, if I am absolutely ignorant of the nature of God? It is clear that we must examine this preliminary question further.

In the course of this section dealing with the attributes of God, we shall point out certain parallels or comparisons which may be drawn between the conclusions of philosophy and the data of Revelation. In this fashion the reader who is interested in theology will be able to see more easily the ways in which our natural and our supernatural knowledge of God agree with and differ from each other.

CHAPTER I

THE PROBLEM OF OUR KNOWLEDGE OF GOD

§ 1. *Attributes which are Contained Explicitly in the Proof for the Existence of God*

THE existence of the Infinite Being is revealed to us through a process of metaphysical inference. We have first to determine what the conclusion to this proof can tell us about the nature of God. We have seen that, upon completing our proof for the existence of God, we know Him by means of four concepts: as *being,* as *absolute,* as *infinite,* and as the *cause* of the finite.

Two of these four concepts are positive (being and cause), the other two are negative (the absolute and the infinite, that is, the non-relative and the non-finite).

The positive concepts by which we represent God are concepts which are *common* to both the finite and the Infinite, because the finite is also being and it can be a cause. The negative concepts which we use to characterize God give us a *distinct* knowledge of Him because He alone is absolute and He alone is infinite. For that reason our knowledge of God includes no concept *which is both distinct and positive at the same time.* None of the human concepts which are implied in the proof for the existence of God represent the Divine Being positively in what properly constitutes Him, or in what characterizes Him with regard to His effects. When we conclude our proof of the existence of God we do not have any notions which belong to Him in a positive and exclusive way. We do not know in positive fashion "what He is." This is what Thomas wished to express when

159

he wrote: *"de Deo non possumus scire quid est, sed solum quid non est."*[1]

This is the logical consequence of the way we reach God in metaphysics. It was the antinomy between the finite and the absolute which led to His discovery as the reality which transcends the order of finite beings. Hence we reach Him only by way of opposition to the finite which alone forms the immediate object of our knowledge.

To know the proper nature of a being in a positive way, we must either seize it immediately *in itself,* or we must know it by means of a *proportionate image* or representation. This second method will be the more perfect according as the image which is used reproduces the object more exactly. This image may be the proportionate effect of the object (thus, the son is the image of his father), or it can be the proportionate cause of the object (as the father is the image of the son), or it can be some representation of the object (a portrait, statue, photograph).

We cannot use any of these ways to get a knowledge of God. We cannot know Him directly in Himself because we reach Him only by a process of metaphysical inferences. And we cannot know Him by a proportionate image because the finite bears no proportion to the Infinite.[2]

1. *Summa Theologica,* I[a], qu. 2, art. 2, object. 2.
2. This does not hold true for theology, which considers the order of grace or the supernatural order. In that order the beatific vision gives man an intuitive knowledge of God in Himself. Again, in the Holy Trinity, the Son is the perfect Image of the Father. Consequently, to know the Son is also to know the Father by a proportionate, even a consubstantial image. Even in His Humanity the Incarnate Word manifested the nature of God by His holiness of life and doctrine.

§ 2. *The Significance of the Positive Attributes*

The proof of the existence of God gives us, therefore, four fundamental attributes of the Supreme Being: two positive attributes and two negative attributes. Our further knowledge of His attributes depends on our development of what is implied in these basic attributes. This process of development will give two series of derived attributes—the series of derived positive attributes and the series of derived negative attributes. We shall soon see what this attempted development can give us. But before beginning that work, we must discuss an important question of principle and method concerning the exact meaning of these positive attributes.

Here we run up against the objections of agnosticism, which can be reduced to the following basic difficulty. All the positive concepts which we will use to signify the divine attributes have been borrowed from our strictly human knowledge, that is, from our knowledge of the empirical order. In their proper meaning all these concepts represent finite objects. What then is their value when applied to the Infinite Being? When we proved the existence of co-principles in the finite order by metaphysical inference we could still determine something of their nature through an analogy with the objects known by proper knowledge. But when it is a question of the Infinite Being, that is, of a being which is transcendent to the finite, a being which does not have the characteristics of the finite, or a being which is distinguished for us precisely by its opposition to the finite, can we still speak of any proportion or analogy between the finite and the Infinite? Can the finite be said to "measure" the Infinite in any way? Can concepts which are drawn from the finite keep any meaning whatever with respect to the Infinite? For example, when we use the term "good" to express an attribute of the finite and an attribute of the Infinite, does this term keep the same sense? Does it have a common meaning in the two cases? If so, what is this sense and how can we defend it?

Once again the answer to this problem should be sought in our proof of the existence of the Infinite Being.

It is true that all our concepts have a primary function of expressing our experience, and that this experience is always the experience of finite realities. But we know that *certain concepts* (those which represent being and its attributes) *have a transcendental extension,* so that everything which is not nothing can be expressed by these concepts. Now the proof of the existence of God has precisely this result, that it shows us the existence of a Being which was unknown to us up to this time. Therefore, this Being is to some extent expressible and knowable by means of the transcendental concepts.

Furthermore, the transcendental extension of the concept of being, which is at the same time the adequate representation of the concrete, is a conceptual expression of the basic unity of everything which exists and of the adequate similarity which binds all beings among themselves. Now the proof for the existence of God gives us the ultimate reason for this ontological similarity. It rests in fact on the *common participation* of all finite beings in the Infinite Being which is their total cause. Consequently, the resemblance of finite beings among themselves, the "family likeness" which their whole being betrays, results from the more fundamental *resemblance which exists between each finite being and its Infinite Cause.* This resemblance follows from the very nature of causality since the cause necessarily precontains its effect. And when it is a question of a total cause, then the effect is completely and entirely precontained in its cause.

There is nothing in the effect which is foreign to the cause, nothing which is not an "imitation" and "participation" with respect to the cause. In brief, every similarity in the real is based upon the similarity of the finite and the Infinite. And this similarity is a necessary consequence of creative causality.

There is however a certain amount of truth in agnosticism, for there cannot be a perfect or univocal resemblance between the finite and the Infinite. Even in the world of finite things, two concrete beings cannot be perfectly similar as beings, otherwise they would be identified. They are *analogous,* their similarity is *imperfect* or *proportional.*[3] This sort of analogy holds a fortiori between the finite and the Infinite, since we know the Infinite precisely as transcending the finite and escaping the essential defects which characterize the finite. Now this fact implies a very important consequence. In the finite order where we know things properly and positively, we can compare finite beings among themselves and to some extent *measure* one by the other. In the quantitative order we can measure in the strict sense, in other fields in a wider and looser sense, by comparing beings under this or that aspect. Thus we can compare men from the point of view of their intellectual ability, their moral worth, their artistic talent, their athletic prowess; and we can also compare men with animals and plants.

But between the finite and the Infinite no comparison is possible because we do not know the Infinite in itself. We have no positive and distinct knowledge of it. Consequently, the analogy existing between the finite and the Infinite does not involve *any determined proportion* between the terms, that is, one which can be measured either in a quantitative fashion or by means of some comparison. If this is so, how

3. See above, Part I, chap. I, § 3, n. 2.

and to what extent can we use positive concepts to express our knowledge of the Infinite Being?

First, we must show that we can attribute this concept to God because it is implied in the proof of the existence of the Infinite Being. Secondly, we must eliminate any finite realization and every finite modality from the attribute which the concept expresses. We must recognize that the manner of realization of this attribute in God surpasses everything that we can conceive by proper knowledge. This is so precisely because we are speaking of a being which transcends the order of the finite, that is, the order of all properly human knowledge. Thus, for example, we shall state that the Infinite Being is "cause" because this follows immediately from the metaphysical inference establishing His existence. But we shall have to add at once that He is not a cause after the fashion of the finite causes which we know. These are only limited causes which are opposed to their effects, which exercise only a partial, superficial, and merely transforming causality, which co-operate with other causes and so forth. We shall also have to state that the causality of finite beings cannot give us any proper idea of transcendent causality.

In this twofold process which we have just sketched, we can recognize the three traditional ways of deriving the positive attributes of God; namely, the ways of affirmation, negation, and eminence. The last two are basically identical, for the way of eminence merely emphasizes what is already contained in the way of negation. In short, both the way of negation and the way of eminence try to correct the positive attributes by means of the negative attributes. God is *cause*, but He is a cause which is *non-finite, non-conditioned,* and so forth.

§ 3. *Metaphysical Analogy of Attribution*

This resemblance between the finite and the Infinite, between the creature and the Creator, is the foundation of our metaphysical knowledge of God. This resemblance throws new light upon the similarity which finite creatures have among themselves. It will enable us to complete the doctrine of the analogy of being developed at the beginning of metaphysics.[4]

The analogical character of the concepts which we attribute to the finite and to the Infinite can be represented by a proportionality in the same way as we represented the analogy of concepts attributed to several finite beings. Being belongs to God more or less as it belongs to Socrates or to the dog Dundee.

$$\frac{being}{Infinite} \text{ more or less } \frac{being}{Socrates} \text{ more or less } \frac{being}{Dundee}$$

But we know now that analogy is based upon *participation,* that all finite beings proceed from the Infinite Being and, therefore, "share" something of His full perfection. From this it evidently follows that the analogy of the finite and of the Infinite implies a *principal analogate* and *secondary analogates;* that is, one of the terms of the analogy, the Infinite, possesses the analogous attribute in a primary and principal way, while the others possess it only in a secondary and derived way because of their relation of dependence upon the first.

Saint Thomas reminds us that in the order of knowledge the principal analogate is the finite being in this sense that our concepts designate first and properly finite objects. Our

4. *Ibid.*

concepts can legitimately designate the Infinite only in an improper and analogical sense by reason of the metaphysical inference which shows us that the Infinite is the total cause of the finite.

This analogy of the finite and Infinite is often called an *analogy of attribution*. We can keep this terminology provided that we stress the essential difference existing between *metaphysical* analogy of attribution and *ordinary* analogy of attribution.

The classical example of analogy of attribution is that of health. In its proper sense the concept "health" designates a quality of the living organism, a certain internal balance resulting from the good constitution and proper functioning of the organism itself. When we say that food or a person's complexion is "healthy," we use the term in an improper or analogical sense. We attribute health to the food which maintains it, and to the color which manifests it. We do not in any way claim that the food or color are healthy *in themselves,* but we merely wish to state that they have a *relation* to health. In this case there is question of an analogy of *extrinsic* attribution, resting upon a relation between the secondary analogates and the principal analogate which alone possesses the quality at issue in an intrinsic and formal way.

However, the metaphysical analogy of the Infinite and finite is an analogy of *intrinsic* attribution because the secondary analogates possess the analogous quality intrinsically and formally, even though they possess it only by reason of the causality uniting them to the principal analogate.

§ 4. Conclusions

This study of our metaphysical knowledge of God leads to very important conclusions.

1. The metaphysical proof of the existence of the Infinite Being already implies a certain analogical knowledge of God, a knowledge which is expressed in terms of four basic attributes, two of which are positive, the other two negative.

2. Further knowledge of God depends on whether we can develop the implication of those basic attributes.

3. The *negative* attributes alone provide a distinct knowledge of God.

4. The *positive* attributes have a knowledge value which is real, but analogical. This value is based upon the ontological resemblance between the finite and Infinite. But these attributes must be corrected by means of the negative attributes.

5. Here as everywhere in ontology we must guard against confusing our human concepts with the reality of which they are only a very imperfect expression. Such confusion would completely vitiate the results of our metaphysical reflection because, instead of leading us to a genuine although very imperfect knowledge of the Creator, it would end in our venerating a base idol—our own mental construct.

6. Lastly, our metaphysical knowledge of God is essentially *indirect* and *incomplete*. It is indirect because we can reach the Infinite Being only by a metaphysical inference. It is incomplete because we know Him only as the cause of the finite, that is, to the extent to which He reveals Himself in His effects.

This is why the philosopher who is also a believer finds that the data of Revelation provides a valuable *control* and *corrective* for the conclusions of his metaphysics. But we must understand correctly what Revelation can give, and use this data with care. Research which claims to be truly metaphysical must be careful to use only the methods which are proper to it as such. Accordingly we must try to make a strictly rational derivation of the attributes of God. However, the personal thought of the philosopher is not infallible and mistakes are always possible, especially in the obscure zone of metaphysical implication. Consequently, the metaphysician will find that a knowledge of the data of Revelation can be very helpful from the psychological point of view, for it suggests many valuable points and protects him against making naïve statements and hasty conclusions.

The data of Revelation also has great interest from another point of view. It informs us about features peculiar to the order of grace which God freely instituted as the gratuitous crown to the natural order. This order of grace, and in particular the order of the Incarnation, introduces completely new factors into the relationship between man and God. Problems concerning providence, justice, mercy, divine co-operation in man's activity, problems of sin and liberty, all these take on a very new sense, when seen in the perspectives of the supernatural order centered about the Incarnate Word. If we compare the data of Revelation with the conclusions of philosophy in these matters, we shall see that there exist rather interesting contrasts between the essential metaphysical laws of reality and the conditional arrangements resulting from our having been freely called to the supernatural life.

Chapter II

THE DERIVATION OF THE NEGATIVE ATTRIBUTES

Since we shall use the negative attributes to get a correct statement of the positive attributes, we must try to derive them first. The process of deriving the negative attributes must begin from the two basic negative attributes expressed in the conclusion of our proof for the existence of God. At this point we must try to state more precisely what they mean.

§ 1. *The Fundamental Negative Attributes*

1. *Infinity.—The Absolute is a "non-finite" or Infinite Being.*—We have a proper knowledge of what a finite being is: it is a being which is opposed to others, which is foreign to others, which is limited by others, and which consequently can stand in relation to others, can be influenced by them and perfected by them. All these characteristics of the finite being reveal its basic relation of dependence to a Being which is completely free of these imperfections, which has none of the characteristics of the finite, and which transcends the order of finite beings. The meaning of divine infinity then is clear; it is the denial of all *ontological finiteness*. The Infinite Being is a being which is not opposed to any other, is not limited by any other, is not foreign to any other, even to finite beings, for it precontains them adequately as their total cause. The Infinite Being does not enter into relation with finite beings; it is not influenced by

them in any way; it cannot receive any increase of perfection from them.

Sometimes the divine infinity is expressed in a positive way by describing it as the "fulness of being" in opposition to finiteness or "measure of being." But this way of speaking is only metaphorical, for the term "fulness" merely adds the picture of a well-filled receptacle, or satisfied capacity, to the denial of finiteness.

We must be careful not to confuse the *ontological* infinite, with the *mathematical* or *quantitative* infinite, whether this be taken to refer to continuous quantity (a straight line stretching out to infinity), or to discontinuous quantity (the infinite series of whole numbers).

Infinity is the *first distinctive attribute* of God. It constitutes the "metaphysical essence" of God. Accordingly the Infinite is the first "proper name" of the Supreme Being in metaphysics. Although this thesis does not agree with the view commonly held in the Thomistic school, we believe that it must be accepted. For indeed, the *aseity* or unconditioned existence which most Thomists propose as the first distinguishing attribute of God, is doubtless an attribute distinctive of the Creator, but in the order of our knowledge we do not know that aseity is a distinguishing attribute of God until we have shown that the absolute is transcendent to the finite, that is, infinite. Consequently, infinity is really the first distinguishing attribute of God, the first concept which is needed and which is sufficient to distinguish God from all creatures.

2. *Aseity.—The Infinite is an Absolute or Unconditional Being.*—The entire analysis which we made in ontology tended to prove that the absolute or unconditioned reality whose existence forced itself upon us even from the begin-

ning of our metaphysical reflection should be sought for beyond the finite. The Infinite alone then is *non-relative, non-conditioned, non-dependent, non-caused;* it alone is *necessary of itself;* it alone *exists by itself (ens a se*—thus the scholastic term : *aseitas* or aseity). In short, the Infinite is at the same time the Absolute. Here we have a new metaphysical "proper name" for God.

§ 2. The Derived Negative Attributes

Once we have determined the two basic negative attributes, we can proceed to derive the other negative attributes which are necessarily implied in the first two. This derivation will consist in denying to the Infinite all those characteristics which belong essentially to the *finite as such,* and then all those characteristics which belong essentially to that class of finite beings which we know distinctly, that is, *corporeal beings.*

1. *The Infinite is Immutable.*—The meaning of this new thesis is clear : the Infinite is completely free from the condition of change observable in the world of finite beings. Not only does the Infinite not change actually, but by its very nature it excludes any possibility of change, either in the sense of becoming something which it is not, or in the sense of ceasing to be what it is. In short, the Infinite is indeterminable, imperfectible, and indefectible.

The Infinite is unchangeable because it is not conditioned. We can put the proof in the following way :

Major: Every subject which changes depends on an extrinsic cause.

Minor: Now, the Infinite is unconditioned or independent.

Conclusion: Therefore, the Infinite cannot change.

We must at all costs avoid conceiving this divine immutability in a clumsy, imaginative way, picturing the Infinite to ourselves as a being which would be frozen in immobility, inert, indifferent, paralyzed, incapable of any initiative, and condemned to stagnation in order to save its immutability. At times the thought of philosophers and theologians seems prey to a false notion of immutability. We will find traces of this later on. However that may be, we must hold fast to the principle that the Infinite excludes all change, that is, all "modification." It is impossible for it to become "other"; it can neither wax nor wane under the action of any exterior cause.

2. The Infinite is Simple.—Simple means not composed. Composed signifies that the thing is made up of parts, of elements which are unified *(com-positum)*. The statement of the thesis affirms then that the Infinite excludes all composition and all plurality of component parts.

We know that *every finite being is composed* in the order of subsistence and in the order of activity. We must now show the reverse of the medallion, that every composed being must be finite and that consequently the Infinite excludes all composition.[1]

We can state the proof for the divine simplicity in the following way:

Major: Every composition in a being implies the constitutive composition of essence and existence.

Minor: Now, the constitutive composition of essence and existence implies finiteness.

1. We cannot prove the simplicity of God from His infinity, because we do not have positive knowledge of the Infinite. We must prove God's simplicity indirectly by showing that composition would entail finiteness.

Conclusion: Therefore, every composition implies finiteness.

The major follows from the very nature of every "composition." Every composition implies a non-identity of the component parts, for every composition is a plurality or a diversity which is reduced to unity. Every real diversity or non-identity in being involves the basic metaphysical condition of a composition from a principle of similarity or perfection, and a principle of diversity or limitation. Without this composition we could not avoid the complete identity of absolute monism. This composition in fact constitutes finite being.

The minor presents no difficulty, for it is evident that this constitutive composition of the finite being entails finiteness, since it constitutes the being as finite by reason of its principle of limitation. Accordingly every composition either coincides with the constitutive composition of the finite being, or presupposes it.

We see then that the simplicity of God excludes particularly any sort of composition *among the attributes* of God. These attributes are distinguished in the order of our knowledge because we cannot express all that we know of God in one concept. We use many concepts to signify one and the same simple reality in God, a reality for which we do not have a proper idea.

3. *The Infinite is Unique.—Unicity* means non-plurality. Unicity means unity as opposed to any external plurality or "multiplication" of the same being, just as *indivision* means unity as opposed to internal multiplicity or "division" of the being. The unicity of the Infinite therefore excludes the existence of other beings of the same nature, that is to

say, the existence of other "Infinites." The Infinite is not "several."

This negative attribute follows immediately from infinity, since strictly speaking infinity signifies absence of opposition to any other being, or opposition only to non-being. An Infinite which would be opposed to another Infinite would be a contradiction in terms.

4. *The Infinite is Incorporeal or Spiritual.*—After considering the attributes which belong to the finite as such, we now take up the attributes which belong to the corporeal world. A *body* is an extended reality which is consequently located with respect to other bodies. A corporeal or material being is an extended being, one which is subject to spatial extension. A non-corporeal being or one which is free from spatial conditions, is termed *spiritual*.[2] Body and spirit are contradictorily opposed to each other.

The Infinite is not a body, but a spirit. It is incorporeal or non-extended. For indeed, *extension involves finiteness* on several counts.

(a) Every *composition* implies finiteness. But an extended or corporeal being is composed of quantitative parts. Therefore, an extended being is a finite being.

The major was proven above. The minor follows immediately from the definition of spatial extension: an extended being is a being which is made up of parts external one to the other; these parts are called "quantitative" because they are the foundation for quantity, or for that dimension which can be measured and numbered.

(b) Every *limited mode* of being implies finiteness. But extension is a limited mode of being. Therefore it implies finiteness.

2. The term "spiritual" is taken here in its negative meaning. The question of a more positive definition is not relevant at this point.

The major is evident if we understand what a finite mode of being is : a modality or determination of being *which sets itself against other positive determinations;* that is, one which excludes other positive determinations. We might think at first sight that every modality of being must be a finite mode, but such is not the case. Consciousness, for example, is a modality of being which of itself does not exclude any other positive modality. It excludes only certain negative modalities, certain imperfections, particularly extension. When we define our terms in this way, we realize that only a finite being can be affected by a finite mode in this determined sense, since the Infinite is not opposed to anything.

The minor cannot be denied, for corporeal or extended being is an imperfect way of existing which excludes a more perfect way, that is, self-consciousness. It is quite evident that a perfect possession of self in consciousness is superior to the dispersion in space characterizing the parts of a body. The unity or indivision of a being which is conscious, is incomparably more perfect than that of an extended being. Now the greater the indivision, the more perfect the being *(ens et unum convertuntur).*

(c) Every body is ontologically finite, and it is also *quantitatively finite.* Every thing which exists is distinct or determined. Now a body is distinct or determined by its spatial limits or its finite dimensions. Consequently, every body has spatial limits or finite dimensions.

Only the minor could cause some difficulty. However, we believe that it follows immediately from the very nature of extension and spatial magnitude. For the only way in which an extended reality *as such,* or a quantified object *as such,* can be determined is for it to have spatial limits or a magnitude which is limited and finite, which can be measured and numbered. Indeterminate magnitude is the very symbol of an object which would be undetermined and consequently impossible to think or realize. Perhaps our imagination can represent in a vague way an infinite magnitude, an unlimited space, a multitude which could not be numbered. But our thought can represent only finite magnitude, limited space, or a multitude which can be numbered. Everything which exists is determined, and we can think only of what exists or what can exist. An unlimited body would be a body which was indistinct and undetermined. Consequently, it would be identical to non-being.

Since it is incorporeal, the Infinite is clearly not *localized* or situated in space. Real or concrete space is only the sum total of bodies considered in their actual extension. Abstract space, which is also called imaginary or geometrical space, is the extended, homogeneous, and unlimited medium which the mind fabricates out of the datum of real space. Every body is localized or situated in real space; that is, it occupies a place which is determined with regard to other bodies.

Now it is evident that an incorporeal being escapes all localization by the very fact that it escapes all spatial conditions. The Infinite then does not exist "somewhere." It cannot possibly have any relation of distance with respect to bodies.

5. *The Infinite is Eternal.*—We said above that existence implies *duration* or *permanence.* That which is, in so far as it is, continues to exist.[3] But the fact of becoming, or successive diversity and the change which affects certain beings, suggests the idea of a *successive duration;* that is, of a duration which involves positive irreducible elements which oppose one another as "before" and "after." Also the fact of local movement which presents itself as a continuous

3. See above, Part II, chap. II, § 1, n. 4.

change, gives rise to the notion of a duration which is both successive and continuous, that is, the notion of *time*.

Real or *concrete* time is identical with the continuous evolution affecting the corporeal world. *Formal* or *abstract* time refers to the intellect's measurement of that continuous movement by an arbitrarily chosen unit. As Thomas following Aristotle put it: *numerus motus secundum prius et posterius*. Most of the realities composing the world of our experience are not only subject to continuous evolution or temporal duration, but they are also measured by time because they have a limited duration. Like other things all living beings have an ephemeral duration. They begin to exist at a certain point in time, and they cease to exist at another point. Their existence covers only one part of the time duration. Consequently, a being which is completely subject to time is a being whose duration is subject to a continuous successive evolution limited by two extremes, a beginning and an end.

Once we have defined these notions, we can easily see that the Infinite is completely free from temporal conditions because of its immutability. Its duration excludes all beginning of existence, all succession (whether it be continuous or discontinuous), and all cessation of existence. This unchangeable duration, free from all the limitations characterizing time, is called *eternity*. The duration of the Infinite is an unchangeable present, an unchangeable permanence, an immobile *nunc*.

Let us note that the term "eternity" is also used in a wider sense to indicate a duration which excludes only part of the characteristics of time, that is, either the beginning or the end of the duration. Thus some may speak of a "world which is eternal in the past" to indicate a creation *from eternity* or without any temporal beginning; or we may speak of "the eternity of hell" to indicate a duration which began and which can imply a certain succession, but which will not have a final term.

Scholastics distinguish a third type of duration which they attribute to pure spirits whose activity is not a continuous movement, although it seems to involve a certain succession of acts or a certain evolution. This duration is called *eviternity* or *aevum*.

§ 3. Conclusions

1. *The Significance of the Negative Attributes.*—The negative attributes have the result of stripping away from our conceptual representation of God every property which would be inconsistent with the absolute transcendence which the Infinite Being has to the finite. When we spoke of the divine immutability we already warned against any imaginative representation of these negative attributes. Unless we guard against that mistake, these derived attributes may present God as a being which lacks all variety and movement, or in a word, lacks everything which constitutes the beauty, charm, and interest of things about us. For we say that God is *simple* and *unchangeable,* but in this world that which is simple is ordinarily poor, commonplace, uniform, monotonous, and boring. That which is immobile is often inert, congealed, rigid, cold, insensible, and tedious.

To correct this unfavorable impression, which is so radically false, we must recall that variety and change are goods only in a very relative sense. The goodness and attraction which they have for us results from our natural imperfection. Since we are imperfect, we have to act to perfect ourselves, and activity implies becoming. Human activity by its very nature is highly complex and implies a great variety of objects and movements. Furthermore, our activity never stops, for none of the goods which we acquire by it can satisfy us. They deceive us, we grow weary of them, the more so since they exclude one another, and we soon feel the privations they entail. But would we still be attracted by variety and change if we could free ourselves from the slavery of an activity which is always evolving and could possess all goods at the same time in one simple and unique act? Now by the negative attributes we merely remove from God everything which entails privation, imperfection, and dependence. We know that God possesses in an eminent fashion, as total cause, everything which constitutes the value and attraction of creatures. But we do not have any proper knowledge of His infinite perfection.

2. *The Revelation of the Trinity.*—The revelation of the mystery of the Trinity throws a great deal of light on these negative attributes of God and helps us to a better understanding of them.

We have shown that the Infinite excludes all composition and all plurality. He is *simple* and *unique*. These metaphysical deductions are exact and they remain exact even in the light of Revelation. For the mystery of the Trinity does not involve any composition in God, or any plurality of Infinite Beings. But Revelation does teach us something that philosophy could not even suspect, that is, the existence of a plurality which does not involve composition or mutual exclusion. The Infinite subsists in three Persons, the Second of whom proceeds eternally from the First, and the Third from the other Two; and no one of them is alien or opposed to another since all remain con-substantial. This mysterious and indescribable plurality lies beyond the reach of our conceptual categories which are adapted to the finite world, where every internal plurality is a composition of opposed parts, and where every external plurality is a plurality of beings which oppose one another.

3. *The Negative Attributes in the* Summa Theologica. —In the *Summa Theologica* St. Thomas does not distinguish the derivation of the negative attributes from the derivation of the positive attributes. The order which he follows in deriving the attributes differs somewhat from the order which we have adopted. Any attempt to show the historical origin, the value, and the inconveniences or weak points in his exposition would call for an extended exegetical study. Without getting involved in that, we can look for a moment at the correlative ideas of Pure Act and Perfect Being in his treatise. These occupy an essential place in St. Thomas' derivation and raise a difficulty of considerable importance.

Saint Thomas makes constant use of the notion of Pure Act *(actus purus)* which was evidently taken from Aristotle. But while the Pure Act of the Philosopher had one single meaning, and on the whole coincided with the Unmoved Mover or First Mover, the Pure Act of St. Thomas has two senses which are quite different. It is true that Pure Act always signifies an act which *excludes all potency,* but sometimes St. Thomas is speaking about a potency *in the order of becoming,* as did Aristotle, and at other times of a potency *in the order of existence,* that is, of a principle of imperfection or ontological limitation. In its first meaning then, Pure Act would be equal to the *Immutable* (which is without potency of changing, without determinability). In the second sense, the Pure Act is identified with the *Infinite* (which has no principle of imperfection or limitation, or which is without essence), and with the *Simple* (without any composition between a principle of perfect being and a principle of imperfect being). St. Thomas arrived at his notion of the Pure Act in the dynamic sense by the *prima via;* he arrives at his notion of the Pure Act in the static sense by the *quarta via.* Ordinarily he passes from one sense to the other as if they were equivalent, without taking the trouble to show that this passage is legitimate.

As we have already suggested, we are here face to face with a remarkable attempt to synthesize Aristotelianism and Platonism, the Aristotelian doctrine of dynamism and the Platonic doctrine of participation. By extending the doctrine of act and potency, St. Thomas effects a very close reconciliation between the two philosophies.[4] But is not this reconciliation a bit artificial, or at least a bit hasty? From the fact that a being has no potency in the dynamic order, does it follow immediately that it is infinite and absolutely simple in the order of existence? Not unless we have shown already that every finite being and therefore every composed being, is determinable. This point is not immediately evident. From this point of view St. Thomas' derivation is somewhat weak and ambiguous.

Similar remarks can be made regarding the divine perfection. In so far as it is pure actuality, the divine perfection can be easily reduced to the negative attributes which we have studied. For indeed we cannot say that God is "perfect" in the etymological sense of the term *(per-factum, totaliter factum),* because God is in no sense "realized" or "produced." He can be said to be "perfect" only in a wider sense, in so far as he is the *fulness of being (totaliter ens).* But again, this expression can have two meanings corresponding to the two senses of Pure Act. In the dynamic order, *imperfect* means perfectible, determinable, affected

4. See above, Part II, chap. II, § 4, n. 1, footnote 3.

by a potency of changing. Then *perfect* would mean immutable. Taken in the static order, *imperfect* means deficient, limited, finite, and in that case *perfect* would mean infinite or unlimited. Once again St. Thomas takes it for granted that these two senses of the term *perfect* are equivalent.

CHAPTER III

THE DERIVATION OF THE POSITIVE ATTRIBUTES

A PURELY negative knowledge would be a contradiction in terms, for negation is an act of thought which necessarily supposes a previously affirmed subject. Consequently, every negation presupposes an affirmation. We have shown above that such is truly the case for our knowledge of God, for we affirm God as *being* and as *cause,* even while we deny that He is *finite* or *relative.* The basic negative attributes rest then upon the positive attributes, which they correct by the method of negation and transcendence.

In this chapter we shall first determine further the meaning and significance of the two basic positive attributes. We shall then deduce the attributes which are implied in the first and in the second. We must first show that we are justified in attributing each positive attribute, and then correct the sense of that attribution by means of the negative attributes, employing the twofold method of negation and transcendence.

§ 1. *The Fundamental Positive Attributes*

1. *Infinite Reality.*—As a transcendental value, being evidently belongs to the Infinite, since the Infinite is truly *being,* truly *real,* and truly *existent.* But it does not exist in the way in which the finite being exists. It exists *infinitely,* that is, without limit, without opposition, without relation to any thing *(Infinitum).* It exists absolutely or necessarily,

or by itself, not relatively *(Ens a se)*. It exists *immutably;* it is Pure Act; it is not active, for activity implies tendency, growth, and perfectibility *(Actus Purus)*. It exists *simply,* without any composition *(Esse subsistens)*.

The expressions Infinite Being, Infinite Reality, Infinite Essence, are synonymous. When we attribute the terms essence and existence to the Infinite, they have exactly the same meaning. Both of them signify the basic value constituting the formal object of ontology.[1] There is only a difference of terminology based upon the distinction which we must admit in the finite between existence (the transcendental perfection) and taleity or essence.

2. Infinite Causality or Omnipotence.—The Infinite is the cause of the finite, for it is by its power that the order of finite beings exist. They exist only as depending on the Infinite which is their total cause, as they are its effects. The Infinite then is of such a nature that it has the power, capacity, or potency to raise up or produce finite beings which are distinct from it, which are finite participations of its infinite reality.

But the Infinite is not a cause after the fashion of finite causes. He is an *infinite* cause, and He is not limited in His causality. His causal influx meets no opposition, does not run counter to any resistance or any obstacle because He is absolutely transcendent to all finite causes. He is an *unconditioned* cause who does not depend on anything in His causality. He is an *immutable* cause, for His power knows no growth or weakening. He escapes all the changes which can touch the effect; He does not suffer any "reaction" because of them; He does not change in any way under their influence. The Infinite is an absolutely *simple* cause which does not

1. See above, Part I, chap. I, § 2, n. 3.

exercise His causality by an accidental activity, but by His very being.

This infinite causality of God is ordinarily called the *Omnipotence* of God. This term expresses well the unconditional character of the divine causality. This causality is its own measure; it is not measured by any thing else. It is this causality which fixes the limits of the "possible." Consequently, we should not say, "God can create everything which is possible of itself"; but rather, "Everything that God can create, that is, everything which can be a participation of the Infinite, is possible."

This infinite causality is also called *Creation* in opposition to the causality of the finite being, which merely transforms an existent thing. To create is to give existence to that which does not exist of itself. It is, therefore, to be the total cause of the creature, for to give being is to give everything. Consequently, to create it is necessary to precontain adequately the effect. Only the Infinite can do this. No finite thing can adequately precontain another, because it is opposed to every other finite being.

Is the divine power *inexhaustible?* The usual answer is that no created world can exhaust the divine imitability, for God's effects are necessarily finite, while the divine imitability is infinite. Consequently, an infinite number of created worlds is possible. However, this sort of reasoning seems to stem largely from imagination, and from a quantifying conception of the Infinite. In reality, we have no positive idea of the divine imitability. Accordingly, if on the one hand we have no reason for thinking that our universe is the only possible effect of the Infinite, on the other hand we have no way of showing that something is possible outside of that which is (in act or in potency).

§ 2. *The Transcendental Attributes*

It is now quite easy to derive the attributes which are implied in the first basic positive attribute. They are the transcendental properties. Strictly speaking, we do not have to prove that these properties belong to the Infinite Being, but we must interpret them by the help of the method of negation.

1. *The Attribute of Supreme Distinction or Transcendency.*—Like every being, the Infinite is distinct or determined. But its distinction is incomparably more perfect than that of the finite being, for the Infinite is opposed only to non-being, which means that it is not distinguished from anything by "opposition." It is distinguished from finite beings by "transcendency," because of the absolute transcendence of the Infinite Cause with respect to its finite effects. While God precontains His creatures adequately as their total cause, yet He is perfectly distinct from them because He produces them as "finite beings," that is, as finite participations of the Infinite. Consequently, the concrete reality of the Infinite can have nothing "in common" with the concrete reality of the finite. The Infinite is distinct from the finite not only in the way in which every cause is distinct from the effect, but in the way in which the transcendent or non-finite cause is distinct from its finite effect.

This new divine attribute of transcendency makes it possible for us to solve a problem which was left unanswered in our discussion of pluralism. It also helps us to surpass a first form of pantheism, which we call subsistential monism. In ontology we distinguished in our world of human experience a certain number of "finite individuals," that is, realities which had a natural unity and were opposed to other realities. But at that time we saw that we could not definitely decide whether these "finite individuals" were really *multiple beings,* or whether they all *subsisted in one unique being* as multiple modes of one same subsistent thing. Now, however, in the light of the divine transcendency the answer becomes clear. Finite beings do not subsist in the Infinite as multiple modes of one same infinite subsistent thing; they really subsist *in* themselves, but not *by* themselves. In reality, they form a multiplicity of finite beings, even though they subsist only as participations of the Infinite. They are the effects of the Infinite and are not to be considered in any way as elements which would make up this divine being, for this divine being is absolutely transcendent and free from any relation which would involve dependence of any sort on the finite. Subsistential monism (which holds that only one subsistent thing exists) or subsistential pantheism (which holds that everything is divine in its subsistence, that everything subsists by the very existence of God), is therefore a metaphysical error.

The difficulties which the pantheists raise against the distinction of the finite and the Infinite, come from a quantifying imagination. They picture the Infinite as being a mathematical infinite, as a "fulness" which exhausts all reality, and then they claim that it would be contradictory to "add" the finite to the Infinite. Once we affirm the Infinite, there is no longer any place left for the finite in the realm of existence.

Strictly speaking we could rule out this objection without any further discussion, since it is based upon a pure equivocation, that is, a confusion between the ontological infinite and the mathematical infinite. But to help the objector see his error better it is well to restate the problem of the distinction between the finite and the Infinite. The question is not whether the human intelligence can prove *in an a priori way* that the Infinite exists, and that it can cause finite beings. Men cannot grasp the divine causality and transcendence in positive fashion even when these attributes have been properly proven, for that would amount to understanding the Infinite itself. But since finite beings actually do exist, and on the other hand are unintelligible unless they are caused by an Infinite Being (that is, one transcendent to the finite), then it becomes clear that the finite and Infinite are perfectly distinct as effect and cause, as relative and absolute, as the finite participation and its non-finite or transcendent principle.

To bring out better this important doctrine, let us examine some of the more usual objections proposed by pantheism.

Objection 1. We cannot add anything finite to the Infinite. Reply: If "to add" means to add in the strict sense, then we agree, but we must point out that in that case we are talking on the level of quantity. If "to add" means to affirm the finite being as a participation of the Infinite, then we deny the statement and ask for a proof. Furthermore, we can prove that the proposition is false, since the finite actually exists and involves the existence of a transcendent Infinite Being.

Far from excluding the possibility of the finite, as the pantheists claim, our metaphysical *notion* of the Infinite presupposes and implies it, since we get this notion by reasoning from the finite and in opposition to the finite. With regard to the affirmation of the *existence* of the Infinite, it likewise presupposes the existence of the finite, since we reach the Infinite only as the total cause of the finite.

Objection 2. If God is distinct from me, He is finite since we are then opposed to one another as two positive realities. Reply: Do two positive realities necessarily oppose one another? Here we must distinguish: if they are foreign one to the other, if one is limited by the other, then they will clearly oppose one another. But if one is the total cause of the other, as the second is the effect or participation of the first, then we must deny that there is *properly opposition* between the two.

Objection 3. Some will admit that finite beings can subsist as distinct from the Infinite. But they claim this possibility still does not rule out the possibility suggested by Spinoza, and his hypothesis therefore remains equally plausible. *Why could we not say that finite beings subsist as finite modes of the Infinite which would be the only truly subsisting being?* Reply: Because in that hypothesis, finite beings would be accidents inhering in the Infinite. This cannot be reconciled with the transcendence of the Infinite. Since the Divine Being is not finite, it excludes any relation of dependence with anything whatsoever, and substance is always essentially correlative to its accidents. Since the Infinite is absolutely simple, it therefore excludes all composition of substance and accident. Since the Infinite is immutable, it therefore excludes all determinability, even accidental or modal determinability. If it be said that the relation of the finite to the Infinite is not a relation of inherence, then it can only be a relation of causality between an effect which subsists in itself and its total cause.[2]

2. Against this reasoning it might be objected that in the hypostatic union the humanity of Christ subsists in and by the Person of the Word and yet does not become an accident of the Word. Between "to subsist in oneself" and "to exist as an accident inhering in the Infinite Being," there seems to be a possible intermediary, that is, "to subsist in and by the Infinite." This was Spinoza's hypothesis of a *generalized hypostatic union* in which all finite natures would be like the human nature of Christ. See. A. Valensin, *A travers la métaphysique* (Paris, 1925), pp. 85-88, 125-33.

In reply, we may make here the following observations.

(1) The hypostatic union is not really an "intermediary case" be-

2. *Perfect Unity or Indivision.*—Like every being the Divine Being is undivided, but it has none of the imperfections of the finite. It excludes all composition, and all multiplicity of component parts. Thus we return once again to the absolute simplicity which we already considered in the list of derived negative attributes.[3]

3. *Divine Exemplarity or Similarity.*—Like every being, the Infinite is similar to every being distinct from it, but this ontological resemblance is not the same as the resemblance which the finite being has to other finite beings, nor the resemblance which the finite has with respect to its Infinite Cause. It is the characteristic resemblance of the total cause to the effect which is adequately precontained in it, the effect which is a finite participation of its infinite reality, and an imperfect imitation of the transcendent model. In short, the

tween the creationist and pantheist theses. As a created substance the human nature of Christ is *adequately distinct* from the Infinite, but depends on the Infinite as its cause. Christ's human nature is, therefore, completely subject to the necessary metaphysical law which we are here speaking of.

(2) Revelation teaches us that between this created human nature and the divine Person of the Word there is *a mysterious bond of dependence.* This explains why the human nature of Christ does not have the autonomy characteristic of a person, but is "assumed" by the divine Person of the Word. This unique and mysterious fact has no effect on the findings of metaphysicians. The theologian's interpretation of the data of Revelation must respect both dogma and ontology.

(3) God's free decree alone determined whether the relationship of hypostatic union is unique or whether it is realized in more than one instance. Consciousness of sin is proof enough for most of us that we do not share a divine personality.

3. These attributes coincide because indivision is a negative transcendental attribute. However, it is listed among the derived positive attributes of God because it is deduced from the positive attribute of being.

Note again that, since the divine Persons are *consubstantial,* the plurality of Persons does not endanger either the divine unity or simplicity.

Infinite is similar to the finite as the *adequate exemplary cause* which the finite imitates.

4. *Infinite Intelligibility.*—The Infinite is intelligible like every thing which exists, but it is intelligible in an eminent degree, because it is intelligible by itself (as absolute), and because it is the source and ultimate reason for all intelligibility (as the cause of the finite). Nothing is fully intelligible unless by the Infinite. The Infinite is the supremely intelligible being, in which all paradoxes are resolved. Its mystery does not raise any problem to which an adequate solution cannot be found. It is the subsistent Truth.[4]

It is a necessary corollary to this attribute that the knowledge of the Infinite is essential to the perfection of every finite intelligence, not only because every intelligence has a transcendental capacity, but because we cannot get a full knowledge of the universal order without some knowledge of the transcendent Principle of this order.

5. *Infinite Desirability.*—The Infinite is desirable in so far as being, but it is desirable in an eminent degree: first, because it is desirable by itself (as absolute); secondly, because it is the source of all desirability (since it is the cause of the finite). It is the ultimate explanation of the desirability of every finite being. It is subsistent Goodness; it is the final goal of every intellectual appetite. Only in it can the created will find rest for its tendencies and the perfect enjoyment to which it aspires. This is so because not only is every will a transcendental appetite, but also the moral goodness or the perfection of the finite will consists in the

---

4. Here we are speaking only of the ontological truth or the intelligibility of the divine Being. When St. Thomas asks "Utrum Deus sit veritas" (I ª, qu. 16, art. 5), he is speaking of formal truth, that is, of truth considered as a quality of the intelligence. This question supposes that it has already been proved that God is an intelligent being.

enjoyment of the universal order, and consequently in a
special way in the enjoyment of the transcendent Principle
of that order.

§ 3. The Attributes which are Implied in the Effects of the Divine Causality

To complete our derivation of the attributes of God, we
must now list the attributes which are implied in the infinite
causality. This analysis will prove very fruitful, and our
treatment of this last phase of metaphysics will be of some
length.

When we try to determine all the implications of divine
causality we see immediately that we can develop this topic
in two ways. First, we can ask what the divine causality
itself implies or involves, and secondly, we can ask what the
effect of God (that is, the finite world) shows us about
the nature of its Cause. Here it will be better for us to consider the latter problem first since its solution will also help
us to solve the former.

Our answer to the proposed problem must be determined
by the following general principle: *the perfection of an effect
pre-exists in eminent fashion in its cause*. This principle is
evident, provided that we have an exact understanding of its
meaning.

When we say that the cause precontains the perfection of
its effect, we do not wish to suggest in any way that causality should be conceived as the "transferring" of some perfection which would "pass" from the cause to the effect.
This crude image does not in any way express the mysterious
nature of the causal influx. The expression which we have
used means that for the cause to have the capacity or power
of producing a certain effect, that cause must possess in it-

self a degree of perfection which will be at least equal to that of the effect to be realized. If we deny that point, we make causality unintelligible, because we are trying to explain the more by the less, the more perfect by the less perfect and, in the final analysis, being by non-being.

On the other hand, when we say that the cause precontains the perfection of its effect in an *eminent fashion,* we mean to emphasize that the cause as such is always superior to the effect as such for the good reason that it has priority of nature (and often of time) with regard to its effect. The effect is inferior because it "depends" on its cause. Hence even in the order of univocal causes, that is, of causes which produce an effect of the same kind (as living beings produce others of the same species), the cause as such possesses in an eminent way the perfection which it communicates.[5]

It is understood of course that we take the principle to refer only to those relations which exist between the *cause as cause* and its *effect as effect.* For if a being is only the partial cause of another being, then obviously it will precontain that being only to the exent of its causal influx upon it.

After stating this general principle, we can now apply it to the Infinite, since this is the total cause of the finite. Hence we affirm that the whole reality of the finite being is precontained in an eminent fashion in the Infinite. Thus it appears that the perfections of the finite world provide us with an added approach to knowledge of the divine perfections. Indeed every perfection which is realized in an effect of God will show us something of the eminent perfection of the cause. Up to this point we have been using the *imperfections* and *deficiencies* of finite beings as spring-boards to get to

5. The superiority of the cause over its effect furnishes the ultimate foundation for the duty of reverence which children owe to their parents.

the Infinite. These helped us first to prove His existence, and secondly to characterize Him by opposition to the finite through the derivation of the negative attributes and correction of the positive attributes. We shall now turn to the *perfections* of creatures to learn what they can tell us of the infinite perfections. Our previous reflections at least seem to justify a hope of that sort.

However, closer examination reveals serious difficulties to the use of this method. Light, colors, perfumes, and heat are marvelous qualities found in the material world. Shall we now ascribe them to the Infinite and declare that He is "eminently luminous, colored, perfumed, and possessed of warmth"? We could do so by metaphor; religious literature quite frequently uses metaphors which represents God as uncreated Light, consuming Fire, and so forth. But no one will claim that these expressions should be taken in their *proper* and *formal* sense, because the very nature of the qualities mentioned implies matter, and we know that the Infinite is incorporeal. Consequently, He possesses these qualities only *virtually (in virtute sua)* in the sense that He is capable of creating them. He possesses them also in an *eminent* fashion in the sense that His perfection, which is superior to that of bodies, precontains in a surpassing way every element of perfection implied in light, color, and so forth.

Must we not say the same thing about all the determinations of the finite, with the exception of the transcendental attributes? In other words, can we ascribe to the Infinite *in a formal sense* anything besides the properties which are common to all beings? At first sight it would seem that we cannot, for every perfection, modality, or determination, is only a particular and therefore finite mode of being, a taleity, an essence, a nature. Apparently all we can say is that the Infinite precontains them virtually and eminently, but that it is impossible to attribute them to Him in their formal sense. If such be the case, it would seem that the new method which we believed we had found must be completely unavailing and impracticable. It would seem that the perfections of the finite can doubtless give us some idea of the unfathomable riches of the Infinite Cause, but apparently they cannot show us any perfections which would be formally attributable to the Infinite, except perhaps the transcendental attributes.

But these difficulties are more apparent than real. Our critique of them will help us to reach the roots of the problem of analogy. The key to their solution is the following: it is not exact to say that all the modalities of being which we grasp in the world of our experience represent modes which are essentially finite. Nor is it exact to say that they have only a purely negative and restricting significance with respect to our knowledge of being as such. To claim that, would be to forget that our human mind grasps being as such only by a concept whose *explicit* content is extremely poor, and which therefore does not in any way reveal to us the infinite "density" or infinite "richness" of the real. To unravel the supremely confused comprehension of the concept of being, we must necessarily appeal to *experience*. We get to know something of the inexhaustibly varied modalities of the real, and the multiple aspects of existence, from experience. It is simply not true, then, that a particular modality of the real gives us only a restriction of our knowledge of being. On the contrary, the meaning of every modality of being which we find in our experience contains two elements or two aspects: a *negative* aspect, for this modality of being is always a taleity, an essence, a particular finite nature which is opposed to other particular natures (we never have the experience of the Infinite); and a *positive* aspect, because this modality of being serves as a new manifestation of the richness of the real. It is the authentic revelation of a positive and original perfection of the universe. To know that being can be "light," "color," "melody," "perfume," "thought," "love," "suffering," and so forth, means in reality to know better the "possibilities," "treasures," and "value" of being. In brief, then, we must distinguish between the *order of being* and the *order of our knowledge*. In the real order it is true that if we compare any finite modality of being to the Infinite, that is, to Being without "essence," then it is only restriction or limitation. But in the order of our knowledge every modality of being gives to us a further valuable precision of our first extremely confused grasp of being.

Seen in the light of this analysis, the problem of our knowledge of God by means of created perfections can be easily solved. The perfections of creatures, that is, the modalities of being which our knowledge of creatures shows us, can and should be attributed formally to their Cause, but only *in the measure in which this is justified by the method described above*. We must justify the attribution itself, starting from the proof of the existence of God. We must correct this attribution by the methods of negation and transcendence. Thus we shall pass from the proper sense of the attribute to its analogical sense. Now while the first of these conditions is always realized (since the Infinite pre-contains eminently the perfections of the finite as its total cause), we find that the second will not be realized as often as it is a question of perfections *essentially bound to finiteness*. For in this case we see that it is impossible to dissociate in this finite modality of being the positive element and the negative element which we discern there.

This leads us to a distinction which is most important in

this connection—that between *mixed* perfections and *simple* perfections.

The mixed perfections are those modalities of the real which are essentially mingled with imperfection, that is, which involve finiteness by their very nature. Thus, for example, "color" is a mixed perfection, because we cannot conceive color without extension. Color therefore can affect only a body, a finite being. When we try to purify the notion of color from every material bond, it loses its formal content; it becomes an empty notion. In the same way "activity" is a mixed perfection because it is becoming, growth, increase of being. All these imply finiteness. The Infinite cannot be "active" in this sense. When we try to eliminate from the notion of activity every bond to the finite (namely, that it is a tendency, second act, act as distinct from existence), we see that the notion loses all content.[6] These mixed perfections, then, cannot be attributed to God in a *formal* sense; God possesses them only *virtually* (in His potency). They are not capable of receiving an analogical sense which could be applied to the Infinite. They can be attributed to God only in a purely metaphorical sense.[7]

6. Many authors take the term "activity" to signify "causality." Taken in this sense, activity is a simple perfection; we can, then, speak of divine activity. Other authors use the term "activity" to signify the divine thinking and willing, by analogy with our immanent spiritual activity. However, this way of speaking is not exact, for the analogy does not bear on the activity as such, but rather on the thinking and willing.

7. Holy Scripture uses a large number of metaphorical expressions and especially anthropomorphic expressions when it speaks about God. Metaphor is also constantly employed in sacred eloquence, poetry, and devotional writing. In spite of its obvious inconveniences, this use of metaphor has great psychological value, for while it does not exactly express the eminent perfection of God, it is still far more graphic than purely metaphysical concepts. Thus expressions like "the uncreated Light," "the Sun of men's minds," and so forth, are much more descriptive than "the Supreme Intelligible."

Simple perfections, on the contrary, are those modalities of the real which are not essentially bound up with finiteness. In them we can dissociate the positive element from the negative element which they imply. Take, for example, "consciousness" or knowledge of self, the unique possession of oneself which formed the starting point for all our investigations.[8] Now it is certainly true that *my* consciousness is a finite modality of the real; that it is a reality which is limited, changing, dependent, and tied up with accidental activity. But I do not in the least destroy the notion of consciousness by freeing it from all these finite conditions. Rather I purify it and elevate it to an infinite degree by conceiving a consciousness which would not be limited nor perfectible, but which would be independent and subsistent. Since the Infinite could not be the total cause of this simple perfection without possessing it itself in an eminent degree, we can conclude that consciousness as such should be attributed to the Infinite in a formal though analogical sense.

In our world of human experience it is not too difficult to determine the simple perfections. As a matter of fact we have a twofold experience; my experience implies an experience of the corporeal world and an experience of the conscious self. My experience of the corporeal world is completely affected by extent or spatial extension. Sensible intuition is inconceivable without this. Every object I experience is a corporeal object, and every modality of the real which objective experience gives me is affected by extension. Consequently, this kind of experience can only give us mixed perfections. It is only our personal experience of the self, then, which can give us simple perfections, when this experience bears upon the immaterial or spiritual elements of my activity. In brief, the only simple perfection accessible to us

8. Van Steenberghen, *Epistemology*, pp. 78-87.

is the perfection of *consciousness* or *personality;* a perfection made up of thought and will, of knowledge and love. But this simple perfection is quite sufficient for us and meets our needs. It has an immense significance, because it opens the way to one of the most striking discoveries in ontology, that of the divine Personality.[9]

1. *Infinite Consciousness.*—Intellectual knowledge or thought is a certain modality of being which I find in myself as an original and irreducible datum of my consciousness. It presents itself as a certain possession of being. This modality of the real does not imply any imperfection or limitation which would be essentially connected with it. It should therefore be attributed to the Infinite in a formal sense. Hence we must conceive the Infinite as a being which *knows intellectually,* an *intelligent* being, capable of seizing and possessing that which is. The Infinite should be conceived as a being which *thinks,* as a being which is *conscious,* because thought implies knowledge of oneself or consciousness. In brief, the Infinite should be conceived as a *mind,* which term is here taken in its positive sense as synonymous with "intellectual consciousness."

But this attribution of thought to God must be corrected with the help of the negative method. The Infinite must not be looked upon as a *limited* thought, that is, as one which would be opposed to anything whatsoever, for example, to its object. Nor should we consider it as a thought which would be *dependent* and *perfectible,* subordinate to its object, and needing to inquire. Nor can it be taken to be an *accidental* thought which would be the act of some faculty, or as

9. This reflection forms the basis for the traditional distinction between the *vestigium Dei* and the *imago Dei.* Corporeal beings are only "vestiges" of God; they cannot really disclose His infinite perfection to us. The spiritual soul of man, however, is an authentic image of God.

a thought which would be developed by a multiplicity of successive acts. The Infinite is, therefore, a thought which is *identical* to the perfect or unlimited being. It is a thought in which subject, act, and object are *identical;* a thought which is one and simple, immutable and perfect; a thought which is perfect immanence, a *subsisting* thought.

We can note that St. Thomas tries to prove that God is an intelligent being not by way of creative causality, but by starting from the divine immateriality, because for him immateriality is the formal reason for knowledge.[10] This method does not appear to be completely satisfactory. It is true that immateriality is a *necessary* condition for knowledge, but it is not quite clear that it is the *sufficient* condition for knowledge.

Most great thinkers have recognized that the supreme Being has the prerogative of thought. The Pure Act of Aristotle was "thought which thought itself," an entirely acceptable opinion. Almost all the great modern philosophers from Descartes to Bergson have recognized the existence of of a transcendent Mind at the origin of all things. And we hardly have to add that Jewish, Christian, and Arab thinkers bear the same witness.

2. Infinite Enjoyment.—In my human consciousness, intellectual knowledge is always accompanied by an intellectual appetite or the will. It is my intellect's imperfect possession of the real which arouses in me the desire to possess that reality better, because this possession appears to me to be a good or a value. I enjoy this good in the measure in which I possess it. Man's act of the will, then, is in turn a *tendency* or *desire* when the good is still absent, *hope* when the good desired appears to be accessible in spite of obstacles to be

10. *Summa Theologica,* I^a, qu. 14, art. 1.

overcome, *enjoyment* or *delight* when the good is possessed. Enjoyment is the perfect act of the will; the love of complacency is the perfect form of love.[11]

Now intellectual enjoyment is clearly a simple perfection, just as intellectual knowledge is. Hence it must be attributed to the Infinite in a formal sense. The Infinite should be conceived as a being who *enjoys* his own supreme perfection, who possesses *beatitude* in a supreme degree, who loves in an inexpressible way his own goodness and delights in it.

Once again, the methods of negation and transcendence must correct the above attribution. The divine will must not be looked upon as a *finite* will, which sets itself over against its subject and sees its desires crossed by various obstacles. Nor should it be looked upon as a *dependent* and *perfectible* will, whose proper act would be desire or hope. Nor should it be looked upon as a will which could be faulty, which would be subject to fear, despair, or sadness. Nor should it be looked upon as an *accidental* faculty which would be the source of many successive acts and capable of adopting contradictory attitudes, depending upon external circumstances. Nor should it be looked upon as a will which would be exposed to any perversion or subject to the influence of errors, passions, or instincts. The Infinite is therefore an enjoyment which is identified with perfect Being and with perfect Thought. It is an enjoyment without limit, without any extrinsic conditions, one which is perfectly autonomous; a will which excludes all the imperfect acts of the will (desire, hope, fear, sadness, and so forth). It is a simple and unique complacency in which subject, act, and object are identified.

11. Van Steenberghen, *op. cit.*, pp. 154-56. According to the terminology used by St. Thomas (*Summa Theologica*, I³, qu. 20, art. 1), *love* denotes in a general way the reaction of an appetite when its object, the good, is present.

In short, the Infinite is *subsistent* love or *subsistent* beatitude. The divine will is the Divine Being in so far as it is enjoyment of self.[12]

3. *Perfect Life or Absolute Immanence.*—If we take "life" to signify the kind of immanent movement or activity which characterizes living things in this world, then life is a mixed perfection which would belong to God only in a metaphorical sense. But the term "life" can be taken in a wider sense to designate simply the *immanence* or immanent character of any act at all. Then thought and will are called living acts in so far as they are and remain immanent to the subject. When taken in this sense, life is a simple perfection, and it belongs to the Infinite in a formal way because He is in a supreme degree immanent thought and enjoyment.

It is clear, then, that the divine life is infinite immanence, implying no reserves or restrictions, no dependence or change.

4. *Infinite Personality.*—The spiritual individual is called a *person* because he possesses the attributes of individuality (unity and autonomy) in a surpassing degree. Consequently, we can say that he is an individual of special rank and exceptional qualities. The prerogatives of the person are shown and expressed in the spiritual activity of thought and free will. These make the person a value in himself, an inviolable being, one who enjoys rights but is also responsible.

12. For the time being we need say no more about the divine *liberty*. Liberty is the autonomy which is proper to the will, its independence from external factors which could influence its actions. Thus defined, liberty does not exclude necessity. The divine will is supremely free because it is not conditioned. But there is nothing "optional" or "contingent" about the divine enjoyment. It is necessary like the divine being itself. We shall come across other aspects of the divine liberty later in our study.

Personality is the immediate consequence of thought and will. It is a simple perfection and it expresses for us a new attribute of the Infinite. It characterizes the Divine Being in so far as it is supremely autonomous, the supreme value and end in itself.

Since the divine personality is infinite, it excludes all the imperfections of created personality. Hence we cannot properly say that God is "a subject of rights," or "responsible," or "a subject of duties." For all these moral and juridical qualifications imply relations of dependence among persons, while the Infinite excludes every relation of dependence on anything whatsoever.[13]

Certainly the derivation of these simple perfections constitutes a positive step forward in our knowledge of God. I am capable of thinking and loving; I am a conscious being; I am a person. My dignity consists in this. Because of this an abyss exists between me and matter; because of this I am capable of the Infinite; because of this I have my own value and my own destiny. The Infinite, which is my total cause, possesses in Himself these attributes to an eminent degree. My thought is only a weak reflection of His thought. My willing is only a distant participation in His love and His beatitude. Can we speak of "personal" relations between the Infinite and myself? Or does His transcendence put an impassable gulf between the Infinite Consciousness and the finite consciousnesses which are its effects? This is the new problem which must now engage our attention.

13. By showing that God is thrice personal, the mystery of the Trinity obviously does not oppose the metaphysical affirmation of the divine personality. Quite the contrary!

§ 4. *Attributes which are Implied in the Divine Causality as Such*

We have studied the divine causality considered as a fundamental attribute which is explicitly contained in the conclusion to the proof of the existence of the Infinite.[14] Now we have to express more clearly what this fundamental attribute implies, or what we can derive from it. We will make this new derivation in the light of the conclusions flowing from our examination of the simple perfections. These conclusions will allow us to state two important characteristics of the divine causality or the divine power; namely, that this causality is *conscious* and is *voluntary*. In this way two new attributes of the Infinite will be brought out—the divine *knowledge* and the divine *benevolence*.

1. *The Infinite is a Conscious or Intelligent Cause.*— Since God is subsistent thought or perfect consciousness, His power, which is identical to His Being, is necessarily conscious. God knowing how creatures can imitate or share in His divine being, knows Himself as the exemplary cause of the finite. He knows His power and His will to create an order of finite beings. He knows that He creates; He is conscious of causing the world. Now just as the divine *consciousness* is the awareness which God has of Himself, so the divine *knowledge* is the awareness which He has of His effects or of His creatures.

But the divine knowledge transcends all finite or limited knowledge. Hence it is not a limited knowledge for which things might be mysterious and impenetrable, nor is it a knowledge which could acquire its objects only with great

14. See above, Part III, chap. III, § 1, n. 2.

effort, nor is it a knowledge which could only gradually en-
large its field of information. It is not a knowledge which
would be *conditioned* by its object, or by anything at all
outside the knowing subject. It is not a perfectible knowledge, subject to the ebb and flow of human awareness. It is
a knowledge which is infinite, as the divine power is infinite.
For by knowing His power which precontains adequately all
its effects, God also knows these effects adequately. It is a
knowledge which is *unconditioned and perfectly immanent*.
Its object or immediate term can only be the divine power or
the divine Being itself, for the divine knowledge cannot be
"received" or "acquired"; otherwise it would be dependent
on created objects. God knows the world in knowing His
power. He knows all *in Himself* and *by Himself*. We cannot say that God knows the world because the world exists
and is "given" to him as an object to be known, but rather
we must say that the world exists because God knows it
and wills it by a perfectly immanent knowledge and will. In
the words of St. Thomas: *Alia a se videt non in ipsis, sed in
seipso;* [15] and again: *Scientia Dei est causa rerum.* [16] Finally,
the divine knowledge is immutable and eternal because it is
unconditioned.

This completely immanent character of God's knowledge
has important connotations in epistemology. Here we have
a knowledge which by reason of its transcendency and perfection is entirely *a priori* and entirely *subjective* in the sense
that the knowing subject is the only norm, basis, and guarantee of it. Here there is no distance between the subject
and the immediate object, for they are identical. Furthermore, with respect to the mediate object (the creatures taken
in themselves), there is no possibility of error or ignorance,

15. *Summa Theologica,* I³, qu. 14, art. 5.
16. *Ibid.,* art. 8.

because it is this divine knowledge which causes the creatures and determines what they are. This "divine subjectivism" is the ideal knowledge and the eminent model for all knowledge. Let us note well, however, that from another point of view this knowledge is supremely *objective,* because it implies complete submission to its object and is in no way a production of its object. The power of God is the only immediate term of this knowledge. God knows that power such as it is by a pure consciousness of Himself and by a pure possession of Himself. Here subject and object are perfectly adequate, indeed identical. As far as the mediate objects of divine knowledge are concerned, God knows them also *such as they are,* because they are what He wishes and causes them to be.

Aristotle saw clearly that the Pure Act excluded any knowledge which would be obtained by the assimilation of objects. But since he had not arrived at the notion of the creative cause, nor at the notion of a knowledge by causality, he had to deny that the Pure Act had any knowledge of the inferior world. In his eyes a knowledge of this sort would have been a defect, for he held there are some things which it is better not to know. On this point, Aristotle's philosophy is quite deficient, and the principle to which the Philosopher appeals to excuse the ignorance ascribed to the First Mover is erroneous. Knowledge as such is always enriching, never degrading; the knowing subject raises the object to the level of his own perfection, since every act of knowledge is immanent. Sometimes it might be preferable not to know certain things, because human weakness might tend to desire them in opposition to the moral law. But this reason is quite outside the order of knowledge as such.

As long as we restrict ourselves to general principles, the question of divine knowledge does not present any special difficulties. But it becomes much more delicate when we consider it in relation to the liberty of creatures. This particular problem has caused rivers of ink to flow and has provoked century-long controversies among scholastics, controversies in which purely theological questions are often confused with metaphysical problems. In our treatment we will leave aside completely everything which concerns the order of grace and those questions which involve supernatural interventions by God. We will confine ourselves strictly to the philosophical aspect of the problem.

(a) *God's knowledge of our free acts.*—The central problem is: does God know *future free* acts and how? We must try to determine whether God knows from all eternity free decisions which do not in any way exist at the present time. If God does know future free acts in this way, then it seems evident that He can know them only in Himself by knowing His own causality. But how then can such decisions still be called "free"? Would they not seem determined from all eternity in the divine causality? And if God does not know future free acts in this way, would this not seem to imply a certain "ignorance" in God? Would we not have to admit that God acquired new knowledge when His free creatures make decisions?

Moreover, the difficulty concerns not only future free acts but *every* free act. Does God know the free act because this act exists, or does the free act exist because God knows it and causes it? Is God's knowledge of man's free act antecedent or consequent? One solution, based on an appeal to the divine eternity, holds that God knows future free acts because for Him there is no past nor future. Both past and future are eternally present to His divine thought. God sees them in somewhat the same way as a man, standing on a hilltop, would at the same time see all the sections of an army passing the foot of the hill. Such an observer would have a simultaneous view of the sections which had already passed the hill, those which were actually at the hill, and those which were still to approach the hill. However, some object that this comparison is weak because all the sections of the parading army exist at the present time. The comparison skips over the difficulty peculiar to the futures, that they do not yet exist. Again, the comparison implies that the observer sees the section of the army *because they exist* and *are given to him*. This ignores the difficulty inherent in liberty. The soldiers' present free acts do not cease to be free because someone sees them. On the other hand, the future free act is an act which in itself will only exist at some future time. It would seem, then, that such an act can be "present" to God only if God knows it by knowing His own causality. Then the whole problem remains whether such knowledge can be reconciled with the creature's liberty.

The basic problem concerns the relation between the *causality* of God and the *liberty* of the created person. Our stand on that problem will in fact determine our views on God's foreknowledge. Any chance of succeeding in our inquiry will depend upon careful definition of our terms: divine causality, liberty.

We have seen above [17] that the divine causality is a total or creative causality. God gives the creature existence, and by giving existence He obviously gives it everything. The creature subsists, then, in continuous dependence on God: it is by this permanent dependence that the creature is what it is, a principle of activity, and can in co-operation with other secondary causes produce secondary acts. But though it is subject to the continuous influence of the Creator, the cre-

17. See above, Part III, chap. III, § 1, n. 2.

ated substance nevertheless is genuinely active; it is really the substance (not God) which acts, and which places the secondary act. If we deny this, we fall into *occasionalism* and place liberty in mortal danger. The immediate term of the creative action is the *created substance* which receives constantly, together with existence, the active power of expanding its being or producing its secondary acts. Thus, everything in the creature depends on the First Cause, but not in the same way. The substance of the creature depends directly on the Creator, while the secondary act depends on Him through the intermediary of the substance.

Note

In what does our liberty consist? In the section on divine enjoyment we said that liberty consisted in the *autonomy of the will*. It signifies that the act of the will is exempt from every extrinsic agent. In the case of a determinable will, that is, of a will which is a power of willing or a will whose act must be realized, then liberty consists in *self-determination* or the power which that will has to determine itself. When different courses of action present themselves to this determinable will, liberty becomes a *liberty of choice*. Finally, if the choice to be made lies between a good action and an evil action, then liberty of choice also involves *liberty of doing evil*.

Is man free? In what sense is he free? If I examine critically the functioning of my own will, I see that my will is not subject to the laws which rule the actions of fixed essences and natures. Properly speaking, my act of willing is not determined either by the action of exterior corporeal agents *(libertas a coactione)*, or by my own nature and its instinctive tendencies *(libertas a necessitate naturali)*, or by the weight of conscious motives which solicit my consent *(libertas a necessitate psychologica)*. But then what determines my will when I place an act of volition? I am aware that I determine myself. Consciousness tells me that it is the concrete self alone which determines my free acts. I make these choices. I am conscious that I am entirely responsible for them. In short, when I place an act of will, I determine myself. The power of *self-determination* involves a genuine freedom of choice, and this implies the possibility of willing evil.

We may agree on this concept of divine causality and on this psychological analysis of liberty, yet a difficult ontological problem still remains to be solved. The concrete self which acts and determines itself is a caused self. It is, therefore, a self which depends constantly on the action of the Creator both for its existence and for its power to act. These two things amount to the same for the finite being. The problem then is: *Does this total dependence mean that my free acts are predetermined in the Creative Cause or not?* If we put more emphasis on divine causality, we will be led to one solution. If we stress rather created liberty, then a quite different solution will be formulated.

The first view is that of *predeterminism*. This position holds that the First Cause precontains in His knowledge, will, and power not only the order of created substances or natures together with everything which results necessarily from their natures, but also all the free acts which created persons place at any moment of time. This view holds that this predetermination (together with foreknowledge which follows as a corollary) is implied in the very notion of creative causality. For, they say, this creative causality is a total causality which must embrace everything, including all the decisions of the creature's will. Many metaphysicians have accepted this view. It certainly safeguards the principle of antecedent divine knowledge or knowledge by causality. But other authors claim that predeterminism reduces the liberty of the creature to a very relative kind of liberty indeed. It is true that liberty might remain complete on the level of secondary causes, but there would be no liberty at all in the relation of the secondary cause to the First Cause.

It is said that this view would entail the following consequences. What I am at any instant of my concrete existence, I am because of an eternal and infallible predetermination. The universal order and all its defects, and the actual history of the created world, would pre-exist completely in the Creative Thought. God would precontain all effects down to the last detail, and so far as He was concerned, there would be no difference between the free acts and the necessary acts of creatures. The history of the universe would be only the inexorable unrolling of the plan already fixed by God in all its details, and the worst crimes committed by created persons would be known, willed, and caused by God before they were willed by secondary causes. (Of course, they would not be willed by God for their own sake, but rather as elements of the universal order, and they would be subordinated to the purposes of the whole.)

The reaction to predeterminism and its implications produced the view which we call *indeterminism* which attempts to safeguard the creature's liberty and responsibility, since these are the indispensable bases for the moral and religious order. This position requires a somewhat more flexible statement of the doctrine of divine causality and the connected divine attributes. It believes that God's omnipotence finds its highest expression in the creation of persons who are truly free, truly capable of determining themselves and of fixing their own destiny; and only thus is the possibility of moral evil explained. Unless in fact we want to impute moral evil to God we must say that it is the fruit of the created will alone. This opinion holds that the way a truly free being will act is by its very nature absolutely unforesee-able, since it is not determined in any way in its causes, and consequently it would be a contradiction to say that this factor could be known apart from its actual realization. It follows that if God creates beings who are really free, then He Himself deliberately introduces something contingent and unforeseeable into His own handiwork. God's supremely free decision meant that free creatures, able to accept or refuse, would write the history of the world under His watchful eye. But does not this view jeopardize the perfec-tion of God by admitting a certain "ignorance" in God? Does it not weaken the divine immutability by recognizing a certain "progress" in God's knowledge? Does it not endan-ger the transcendence of God by stating that God depends on creatures for His knowledge of free acts?

Indeterminism answers the problem as follows. There is no imperfection or "ignorance," strictly speaking, involved in not knowing something unknowable, any more than there is impotency involved in not being able to create the impos-sible or the contradictory. On the other hand, we must not take divine immutability to mean the inertness of a block of stone. Immutability excludes from God any change in the strict sense, that is, all acquisition of new perfection or loss of former perfection. Now since the created order is entirely the effect of God, all its potentialities are precontained in eminent fashion in the Creative Cause. Consequently, the fact of knowing the free decisions of creatures does not in any way confer a "new perfection" or genuine "enrich-ment" on God. God knows these acts by reason of His pres-ence in the innermost being of created substances, as their permanent Creative Cause. Knowledge of this sort excludes all passivity and even all receptivity, properly speaking, with respect to the creature. All these difficulties stem from conceiving God's immutability too narrowly and rigidly. Such a rigid conception would in fact render all God's free decisions unintelligible; for example, the decision to create, the decision to create this world rather than another, the decision to call created persons to the supernatural life, the decision of the Incarnation, and so forth. To sum up, indeterminism charges that predeterminism conceives certain attributes of God in too imaginative a way and in so doing really denies to God the power of creating truly free persons.

Authors have employed both these methods in trying to solve the problem of the relationship between God's causality and man's liberty. Many hold that the two methods are irreconcilable, claiming that predetermination denies precisely what liberty asserts, namely, that the created person is autonomous in determining his own will.

But Christian thought has never ceased trying to reconcile man's liberty with God's foreknowledge. (It has not always held that foreknowledge implies predetermination.) The affirmation of man's liberty and responsibility is clearly essential to Christian thought, for without it the ideas of sin, redemption, expiation, and eternal sanction lose all meaning. Christian thinkers and theologians seem to believe that God's eternal foreknowledge of man's free acts is necessarily implied in the transcendence, immutability, and providence of God. They cannot agree that God is a "spectator" of angelic and human history and that God's providence may be conditioned, at least in part, by the free decisions of creatures.

But how can we bring about this desired reconciliation? Some have abandoned the attempt and taken refuge in mystery: "we hold the two ends of the chain (foreknowledge

and liberty), but we do not see how they join. . . ." [18] Others
are not satisfied with so simple an answer. They acknowl-
edge the mystery, but they claim that reason sees a contradiction between predetermination and liberty. How can we
escape this contradiction?

Different attempts at reconciliation have been made in the
course of history. *Bannesianism* proposes the following
solution. It adopts the predeterminist point of view, but tries
to show that predetermination does not destroy the liberty
and responsibility of the creature. The act of creation does
not destroy liberty, but constitutes it. God creates me active,
capable of willing and determining myself. Creation is not
a *motion;* hence I am not "pushed" to will in spite of myself.
This refutes the position of the fatalist who introduces God
into the order of secondary causes, as if God were a hidden
mover giving a definite and irresistible push to the created
will. Indeed, on the level of secondary causes, everything
happens as if creative causality did not exist at all. My free
act is completely my act, but I am also entirely a creature of
God, an effect of God. At the moment when I act, my actual
personality is created by God.

Some critics dismiss the Bannesian theory as a mere
verbal defense of man's liberty. While I write these words,
God knows, wills, and causes in His eternal present, the free
acts of men who will live two hundred years hence. Since
these men do not exist in any way at the present time, they
count for little in the determination ascribed to the First
Cause. The critics ask how any kind of liberty can be pre-
served in Bannesianism. How explain sin which is a rebel-
lion of the created will *against* the Will of God? How
explain the sinner's responsibility *before* God? What mean-

18. Fernand Mourret, *A History of the Catholic Church,* trans. Newton
Thompson (6 vols.; St. Louis: B. Herder, 1931), V, p. 638.

ing could man's "self-determination" possibly retain if it is the infallible result of an eternal predetermination on the part of God? How could we escape a universal determinism and fatalism according to which "all is already written"?

The rival system of *Molinism* tries to avoid the shortcomings of Bannesianism by dissociating foreknowledge from predetermination. God's foreknowledge would be based not on predetermination, but rather on His knowledge of conditional future acts or "futurables." God would foresee what man would decide in any given situation and, in the light of this prevision, would decree the co-operation necessary for man's realization of those free acts. Against this view it has often been objected that a knowledge of the futurables would imply that there is a necessary relation between the free act and its condition. It is said that this would amount to a denial of liberty, for the free act by its very nature is not determined either in its causes or in its conditions.

St. Thomas himself reaches no definite conclusion on this point, and his uncertainty shows the need for caution. Thus the formulas which he uses when speaking of God's knowledge of free acts seem sometimes to incline toward an a priori or antecedent knowledge, and sometimes they suggest an a posteriori or consequent knowledge.[19]

We may certainly say that full light has not yet been thrown on these difficult problems. This is obviously the clear lesson to be drawn from the century-old controversies which they have caused. The Molinists claim to show that the Bannesian view is indefensible, and the Bannesians claim the same against the Molinists. Should not the fact that for centuries so many great theologians have grappled with a

19. This hesitation is rather obvious in the *Summa Theologica*, I³, qu. 14, art. 13. See also the texts collected by A. Grégoire, *Immanence et transcendence*, pp. 195-96.

problem without success, cause us to suspect that perhaps the question has been badly stated? [20] Because of its many theological ramifications, a definite solution is not to be found among the philosophers but among the theologians. We ask them to treat the question methodically, to distinguish clearly between the order of creation and the order of grace, between the natural order and the supernatural order, for this latter order entails a special providence on the part of God which profoundly affects the data of the problem.[21] A meticulous attention to method will emphasize the need of determining just what are the certain data of Revelation in this regard as distinguished from theological opinions.[22]

(b) *Does God know the possibles?* God does not know possibles in themselves because they do not exist, and only

20. J. M. A. Vacant, *Etudes théologiques sur les Constitutions du Concile du Vatican d'après les actes du Concile. La Constitution Dei Filius* (Paris, 1895), I, p. 278. "This," writes Père Vacant, "is one of the deepest mysteries tormenting the mind of man. Theologians have labored to lessen the obscurity, but up to the present their theories have produced more heat than light. Thomists and Molinists accuse one another of destroying either the Providence of God or the liberty of man."
21. A number of important doctrines are connected with this special providence of God; such, for example, are the nature of prophecies; the nature of predestination; the nature and action of grace; the governance of the world, the chosen people, and the church.
22. Revelation contains so many clear affirmations of man's liberty and responsibility that there is no need to cite specific examples. The doctrine of creation which is clearly taught in Scripture was defined as a truth of faith by the Council of the Vatican (*Const. de fide catholica,* cap. I and canons 1-5). The Vatican Council presents divine foreknowledge as an aspect of Providence: "Universa vero quae condidit, Deus providentia sua tuetur atque gubernat, *attingens a fine usque ad finem fortiter et disponens omnia suaviter* (Sap. viii, 1). *Omnia enim nuda et aperta sunt oculis ejus* (Heb. iv, 13); ea etiam quae libera creaturarum actione sunt." According to many theologians, the Fathers of the Council did not intend to *define* the doctrine of foreknowledge as revealed doctrine or as imposed of faith. See Vacant, *op. cit.,* pp. 276-77.
The recent Encyclical *Humani Generis* (August 12, 1950) denounces among theological errors the fact that some refuse to God an eternal and infallible foreknowledge of men's free acts and recalls that this error is opposed to the "declarations" of the Vatican Council.

that which is, is knowable *(ens et verum convertuntur)*.
God knows His power and knows Himself as imitable. But
does He not know an infinity of possibles in His power?
The question again implies a quantitative conception of the
infinite power. Infinite power does not imply in any way an
"infinity" of possible imitations of the Infinite. We can say
nothing more.

(c) *Does God know the futurables?* A futurable is a
conditional free act. Now it is clear that there are conditional determined acts: "If Peter had drunk this poison, he
would have died of it." We know that a certain dosage of
such poison is fatal for every human organism. But here is
an example of a conditional free act: "If Peter had heard
this sermon, he would have been converted." In this case
conversion is a free act related to an event which it is pre-
sumed did not take place. Peter did not hear the sermon
which would have converted him. Following Molina, some
modern scholastics claimed that God knew the futurables,
and they appealed to this knowledge to explain predestination. They said that God would take His knowledge of the
futurables into account in making His eternal decrees regarding the last end of created persons. They called this
knowledge the *scientia media* because this was an intermediary between the knowledge of that which exists *(scientia visionis)* and the knowledge of the possibles which do not
exist *(scientia simplicis intelligentiae)*. They argued that
while the free activity of possible beings was totally indetermined and indeterminable, my futurable acts which by definition will never be realized, are nevertheless determined in
the divine thought. God knows what I would have freely
decided, if I had been placed in a situation in which I actually never will be. Serious objections have been advanced

against this theory from the critical point of view. The opponents of the theory claim that the futurable has exactly the same standing as the possible; *in itself* it is nothing and never will be anything. They deny that it pre-exists *in its cause,* if that cause is said to be truly free. God can know it only in His own power, exactly as He knows any other possible. But even in the divine thought there is no determined relation between the created subject and its futurable acts.

(d) *Does God know the quantitative infinite?* Scholastics have been very concerned with determining how God knew the infinite multitude of possibles, the infinite series of numbers, and so forth. These questions can be reduced to simple fallacies of interrogation because the quantitative infinite cannot exist.[23] Since it cannot exist, it is not knowable even by God. *Ens et verum convertuntur.* Consequently, God does not know the infinite series of whole numbers because it does not exist, and it cannot exist any more than a squared circle. But God knows, as we do, and infinitely better than we do, that no whole number is the last in a series or the greatest possible number, and that the series therefore is "indefinite" or indetermined by its very nature; that is, it is always capable of increase. Why should God know as determined something which always remains essentially determinable?

Traditional philosophy speaks of the *immensity* and *ubiquity* of God to indicate the presence of the Infinite in the universe as a whole. When taken literally, these expressions are really only metaphors because they describe God as being "locally present" everywhere that creatures exist, as being "immanent" to the world after the manner of the

23. See above, Part III, chap. II, § 2, n. 4, c.

Stoic pneuma.[24] When they are reduced to their true meta-physical meaning, these attributes coincide with the divine knowledge. The created universe is wholly present to the divine thought which knows it completely in and by its creative power.

2. *The Infinite is a Çause which is Supremely Benevolent.*—Since the divine enjoyment is identical with the divine being, consciousness, and power, the creative act is evidently a *voluntary* act, or an act of *love,* which is not foreign to the eternal act by which God enjoys His own infinite goodness. If God creates, it is because He takes delight in His own perfection and knows it as the archetype which is imitable by finite creatures. To will to create is to will to communicate His goodness to finite beings, to will that creatures be and that they be good. The will to create is therefore an act of *benevolence,* the result of the delight which God takes in Himself. The divine benevolence is therefore the divine *enjoyment* in so far as it is *efficacious,* that is, in so far as it expresses itself in the will to create a world which will be a participation of infinite goodness.

Divine benevolence has none of the marks of finite benevolence, or of the love of benevolence which we find in a finite will. The will to create is *not limited by anything;* it meets no opposition or resistance because it produces everything which is distinct from God. Nor can we say that the divine will clashes with the free will of created persons, for these persons exist and are free only by the will of God. Conse-

24. It would be more exact to say, following St. Paul, that the world is immanent in God—*in ipso enim vivimus et movemur et sumus* (*Acts,* xvii, 28)—provided that the phrase is understood to express not a relation of inherence, but one of total dependence of the finite on the Infinite. We cannot, however, completely dissociate the notion of immanence from all spatial images.

quently, if they abuse their liberty by willing disorder, these disordered acts do not hinder the creative will in any way.

The will to create is completely *unconditioned*. It does not result from any "inclination" or "tendency" toward creatures as toward an end distinct from the Creator, but rather it flows from the satisfaction which God finds in His own goodness. God rejoices within Himself at His work because it is His participated goodness. The desirability of God's creation is a received desirability: it flows from Him. Creatures are good because God loves them: *voluntas Dei est causa rerum*.[25] The goodness of creatures is not the cause of the love which God has for them, but rather it is the effect of this love, which is a love of complacency for Himself and a love of benevolence for the things which participate in His perfections.

The divine benevolence is characterized by supreme munificence. God does not create in order to increase his beatitude, or to gain advantage from creation. He is absolutely imperfectible, and creation is merely an imperfect participation in His own perfection. God creates because he delights in His own goodness, and because He wishes to communicate it to His creatures.

But did not God create the universe *for His own glory?* This formula is rather equivocal; it runs the risk of being misunderstood. Unless we are careful, it will represent the most liberal, benevolent, and munificent act which we can conceive as something "egoistical" and "ambitious." The true and acceptable sense of the expression seems to be the following: if God creates, He cannot will any good which would be *foreign* to Himself; He cannot realize any world which would not be completely and wholly a participation in and a manifestation of His own goodness. On the other hand,

25. *Summa Theologica*, I^a^, qu. 19, art. 4.

created persons can have no other end than the knowledge and enjoyment of the created order and its uncreated Principle, for the perfection of every intelligence and every will requires the knowledge and enjoyment of the supreme Intelligible and the supreme Goodness. If we distinguish in the perfection of the finite person the *bonum honestum* (the conformity of his will with the real order) and the *bonum delectabile* (the enjoyment which accompanies this conformity), then the *bonum honestum* is evidently the primary element. This being the case, it is impossible that creation could have any other term or goal than the "glorification" of the Creator. For this glorification is merely the recognition of God's supreme goodness by rational creatures. And it is impossible that God could wish anything else than this theocentric order.

3. *The Infinite Freely Creates the Finite World; Consequently, the Finite World is Contingent in a Strict Sense.* — The order of finite beings exists in complete dependence on the Infinite Being as the relative depends on the Absolute. But does the Infinite create the finite necessarily or freely? Does the relative proceed from the Absolute necessarily or contingently? This is the problem which we must now examine.

Very few philosophers have ever arrived at a true notion of creative liberty. Those who arrived at the idea of creation have almost always looked upon creation as an eternal and necessary act having an inevitable effect. Hence the universe is taken to be a *necessary emanation* from the First Cause. This point of view seriously compromises the divine transcendency, and the systems which have adopted it can hardly be called theistic systems, since they must logically end in *emanationist pantheism*. This is a new but very important and very widespread form of pantheism.

Here we have to choose between two opposed conceptions of the universe. According to *emanationist pantheism*, everything is necessary, and the relative is as necessary as the Absolute; but while the Absolute is necessary of itself, the relative derives its necessity from the Absolute.[26] According to *creationism,* only the Absolute is necessary. It causes the relative in a free way. The relative is therefore contingent.

Many philosophers subscribe to the view that if we understand divine liberty to be a *liberty of choice* (to create or not to create, to create one world and not another), then it cannot be reconciled with the simplicity and the immutability of God. According to them this would introduce into God something contingent, something optional, or the possibility of being ordered in different ways. Now the Infinite is simple, and the creative act is identified with the eternal and necessary being of God.

Once again we see that this fundamental objection betrays a gravely inexact notion of the negative attributes of God, and especially of *immutability*. Immutability removes from God the imperfection which is essential to all becoming properly speaking—the imperfection which is essential to all "alteration," to all "becoming other"—because every alteration implies a dependence on something else, that is, an extrinsic cause. Now creative liberty not only does not imply such a becoming, but it formally excludes it because, as we shall see, creative liberty implies the supreme independence of the divine will. The immutability of God is an

26. Pantheists sometimes introduce, quite illogically, a certain degree of contingency into the order of finite beings by admitting that finite persons are free.

obstacle to creative liberty only if we take it to mean in-activity, stagnation, and paralysis.

But is creative liberty compatible with the *simplicity* of God? At first sight it might not seem to be, for either we have to recognise the divine simplicity and consequently identify absolutely the creative act with the eternal and necessary existence of God (in which case this act is no longer free!) ; or we must sacrifice the divine simplicity by saying that God creates by a free act which is distinct from His existence.

Some have tried to solve this difficulty by saying that God creates freely by a necessary act which is identical to His necessary being. But this is nothing more or less than a contradiction in terms, for "to create freely" signifies "to create by a free act." To state then that the created world is contingent, or that it does not come necessarily from God, means that we are obliged to find somehow in God himself the reason why the world exists when it could have not existed. It means, then, that we have to admit contingency in some sense in God, since a cause which was necessary under every aspect could only cause something necessary.

To see that the divine simplicity does not exclude a certain "contingency" in the free decisions of God, we must recall just what this attribute of divine simplicity means. Simplicity excludes from the Infinite Being only that kind of composition which we find realized in the finite being. It is a negative attribute which tells us nothing positive about the inner mystery of the divine Being. Thus we know that the free contingent creative act cannot be *absolutely* identified with the divine Being which is necessary. We also know that this act cannot be conceived as a "second or accidental act," because that would imply a composition of substance and accidents. But, on the other hand, we simply do not have any positive idea of the manner in which the creative act is distinguished from the necessary being of God.[27]

After clearing away these prejudices which could prevent further progress, we must now grapple with the problem more directly and try to show in a positive way that the Creative Cause is supremely free with a true liberty of choice. We can do this either by showing that liberty of choice is *a simple perfection,* or by examining and considering *the nature of the divine causality itself.*

I enjoy liberty of choice regarding the particular goods which vie for the consent of my will. I am not forced to will them either by the action of corporeal beings, or by my own nature, or by my own instinctive tendencies, or by the motives which I see for willing them. I determine myself to will some of these goods rather than others, to will them or not to will them, for none of them appears to me to be absolutely indispensable. It is true that my liberty of choice is imperfect in so far as it involves the liberty of sinning by choosing a good which is not a true good for me as a person, but which merely plays up to some disordered tendency of my complex nature. Apart from that, however, the liberty of choice which I enjoy is the expression of my independence and value as a person. It is the sign of my superiority over the relative and defective goods presented to me. This *prerogative of the person* should belong in eminent fashion to the First Cause, when its will considers relative and optional goods which are not essential either to its perfection

27. The most Holy Trinity provides a striking case in point. We learn that there is a real "plurality" of Persons in God, but that this plurality does not involve either a "composition" among the Persons or a "plurality of beings." Human concepts cannot represent this mystery. Somewhat the same thing holds for the mystery of creative liberty; in which case we can demonstrate the *fact* of liberty, but cannot show *how* this liberty is exercised in God.

or its beatitude. This is evidently so when it is a question of creating or not creating finite beings, or creating these beings or those beings, for no finite being is essential or necessary to the divine perfection and happiness. The creative act is, then, an act which is free with a true freedom of choice. God can create or He can *not* create. He can create this order or that order, provided that the effect corresponds to the requirements of His wisdom, as we shall shortly show.

We can establish the same point more directly by considering the nature of the divine causality itself. We have seen already that this causality is conscious and voluntary. If God creates, He knows that He creates and He wills to create. Now is this act of thought and will free, and in what sense? It is evidently free from any *external compulsion,* because it is absolutely unconditioned and independent. For the same reason it cannot be determined by any motive which would be *alien* to God, or by some external goal which had to be attained. There remains then the hypothesis of an *internal necessity,* a determinism which would be either natural or psychological. But these two forms of necessity cannot be distinguished in God, because God is conscious by nature, and His consciousness is identical with His being. Hence the creative act is of its very essence an act of thought and love. It cannot be a merely instinctive act, nor the expression of a blind causality. If this is the case, then the problem becomes more simple and we should formulate it in the following way: Does the knowledge which God has of His own nature compel Him to create, to produce creatures participating in His nature? Clearly the answer is "No." Since God is infinitely good by Himself, His own infinite desirability is the only necessary object of His will. It alone is the essential term of His satisfaction and His

enjoyment. Since a created universe is only a participation
of this infinite goodness, it cannot pretend to be in any way
essential to the divine perfection, an indispensable complement to the divine nature, or a necessary condition for divine
happiness.[28]

It is superfluous to stress that the liberty of the creative
act must remain mysterious for us. To clear up that mystery
we would have to know God Himself.

4. *The Infinite is a Cause which is Supremely Wise, Prudent, and Provident.*—This attribute adds an important new
detail to our notion of divine causality by removing from
creative benevolence any suspicion of its being a frivolous,
capricious, or senseless act. In short, wisdom acts as a coun-
terbalance and complement to liberty. Even if the creative
act does not have a determining motive, it must have a
motive which is sufficient and worthy of God. For a free
act is also a conscious act, an act of the intelligence, and
therefore an act which is inspired by some motive or some
reason for acting. Creation is optional in the sense that
there is no reason compelling God to create, but it is possible because God has a good reason for creating. What is
this reason? What contribution can creation make which
might be worthy of God?

Creation would not have a sufficient reason if it meant
merely the production of irrational creatures participating in
the being of God. Such participation would be completely
useless and would add nothing to God's beatitude. God's

28. Revelation throws further light on this doctrine. God indeed is essentially Father, and necessarily engenders His Son or Word. This
generation is not through some blind compulsion of His nature but by
an act of thought, and if this act is not free, it is because the Word is,
like the Father, God. Eternal generation of the word is essential to the
divine nature, for the Word is consubstantial with the Father.

consciousness and joy must be shared. In other words, if there was to be a creation at all it had to include one or more persons capable of enjoying created goodness and its uncreated Principle. The world must, therefore, include at least one finite person; otherwise it would be completely devoid of sense. The fact of making one or many created persons who would participate in His goodness, knowledge, and happiness, was for God a *sufficient motive* for creating. And this motive is worthy of God because, on the one hand, a creation of this kind has a value in itself, a sense, an intelligible end, and on the other hand, this value remains completely subordinated to the Infinite Value of which it is but a participation. Hence it does not imply any loss of rights in God, any tendency which has to be satisfied, any new perfection which has to be acquired, or any other love than delight in His own goodness, whether it be considered in itself or in its finite participations.

To determine the purpose of creation, we must distinguish between the *finis operis* and the *finis operantis*. The *finis operis* or the objective end, the positive effect of the creative act, consists in this: one or many created persons participate in the goodness, knowledge, and beatitude of God; or in other words, God is glorified by the happiness of the persons created by Him. The *finis operantis,* or the motive for acting which inspires the Creator, is the love of His own goodness, the essential love of complacency which He has for His own goodness, and the elective love of benevolence which He has for the finite participations of this goodness.

Creative benevolence is therefore an intelligent or motivated act. We call it *Divine Wisdom* in so far as it directs the created world to a supreme perfection, or to a permanent last end. *Sapientis est considerare causas altissimas et ordinare omnia secundum illas.* We call it *Prudence* in so far as it entails a perfect knowledge of the end to be reached and of the means to be used. *Prudentia est recta ratio agibilium:* the correct understanding of what should be done.[29] It is called *Divine Providence* in so far as it disposes all the elements of creation for the realization of the last end to be reached. The entire universe contributes to the perfection of the activity of the finite persons who are part of it. And these persons find in the order of finite beings everything necessary for obtaining their end.

When considered in relation to created persons, Divine Providence manifests still other attributes. It is called *Predestination* in so far as it assigns to these persons the value of ends in themselves, and not merely the value of means to an end. It is called *Justice* in so far as this end is the natural sanction of the creature's own moral activity, whether it be good or bad. It is called *Mercy* in so far as this sanction becomes definitive for the human person only at the end of a period of probation, during which his will always remains capable of "conversion" to the good. Mercy, then, is justice in so far as it takes into account the weakness and fickleness of men. It is called *Sanctity* in so far as it is not affected in any way by the moral evil committed by created persons; "holy" signifies "separated" or "free from stain." The Creative Cause is in no way responsible for or affected by the anarchy of moral evil.[30]

These different facets of Divine Wisdom are often called the *moral perfections* of God, by analogy with the corresponding virtues in man. But this way of speaking is improper, for since God does not strive toward a perfection

29. This was the definition of Aristotle adopted by St. Thomas.
30. The *philosophical* concepts of providence, predestination, justice, mercy, and holiness which we have just defined, should not be confused with the corresponding *theological* concepts which have a far richer significance. See the following footnote.

which He has to realize, He does not have to conform Himself to a moral order as we do. We cannot speak of morally correct or incorrect conduct in Him. He is Himself the only norm of His goodness and the supreme norm of all perfection. He is the First Cause of the moral order.

The discovery that an Infinite Being exists should rouse us to wonder and perchance to admiration. To learn that He is a Person should enkindle our mind still further. And to be assured of God's providence in our regard, should cause our hearts to burn with all the sentiments of religion— adoration, gratitude, admiration, and love. In this way our philosophical analysis ultimately proves that the so-called "God of the philosophers" has all the attributes essential to the God of the great monotheistic religions.[31]

§ 5. Conclusion

Certainly the most important result which ontology can have is that it raises our minds to a metaphysical knowledge of God and His attributes. In spite of its manifold imperfections this knowledge is still most precious to us because of its consequences for philosophy (especially for moral philosophy), for theology, and for our own religious life. Yet we must learn to avoid certain dangerous pitfalls if

---

31. However, we are still far removed from the "God of Abraham, Isaac, and Jacob," and especially far from the "God of Jesus Christ." Revelation does not tell us anything that negates the attributes we have ascribed to the metaphysical Infinite. But what God has revealed to us of His own divine life, of His special providence and love for men as shown in divine adoption by grace, in the Incarnation, and in the Redemption, manifest new and unsuspected attributes of Infinite Being. We have already noted that these divine decisions profoundly modify the whole economy of religion and give a new sense to attributes like providence, predestination, and the justice, mercy and holiness of God.

our knowledge of God is to produce the fruits we should rightfully expect from it.

First, on the level of our philosophical thinking, we must not try to confine God within the poor human concepts which we must use to represent Him to our intellects. Even more so must we distrust the images which always accompany our concepts and which tend to reduce every object of thought to a corporeal object. God's ineffable reality is infinitely more rich, more beautiful, more admirable, and more desirable than we can ever conceive. Think, for example, of the totally inadequate ideas and images which spontaneously arise in us when we say that God is simple, immutable, eternal, that He knows all things "in Himself," and so forth.

We can best remedy these imperfect representations and this lack of "perspective" by cultivating an attitude of *intellectual humility,* a distrust of self, an appreciation of our own intellectual limitations, and a realization of the paltry means at our disposal when we try to get beyond the sensible. This intellectual modesty will make us all the more prudent when we try to express our imperfect knowledge of God. At times we find it more prudent to substitute metaphor for a metaphysical formula which may appear harsh and equivocal. We must also widen our perspective by studying and observing the marvels of creation. In this regard, all the natural sciences can be of great help. For each of them in its own way emphasizes the infinite power, wisdom, and benevolence of God as revealed in His work. Thus we can easily see how the study of the universe, with its prodigious distances, awe-inspiring energies, and unswerving laws of movement, will naturally give men a far better appreciation of the greatness of God than will the mere negative concept of the Infinite.

The Christian thinker must also avoid any tendency toward rationalism and naturalism. The rationalist tendency would limit our knowledge of God to what we can know from metaphysics, neglecting the all important contribution of Revelation. It is true that our metaphysical derivation of the attributes of the First Cause ought to be made in a purely rational way. The clear distinction between the methods employed by philosophy and theology throws into relief the interesting contrast between the "God of the philosophers" and the "God of Jesus Christ." But once we have noted this distinction for purposes of method and critique, let us not forget that we must complete our metaphysical representation of God in the light of Revelation. For Revelation not only gives men new light on the mystery of the deity (the Holy Trinity), but itself forms part of a gratuitous gift which God has made to men in calling them to the supernatural life and fulfilling that vocation in His Incarnate Word. This completely unexpected proof of God's benevolence, this order of grace and the Incarnation, this sort of irruption of the Divine into the sphere of the human, this mysterious insertion of a Divine Person in the history of humanity, entails entirely new relations between men and God and gives a very new sense to certain basic religious values. The Christian thinker must perforce take these things into account and should be very careful when fitting his philosophical views into the Christian synthesis furnished by Revelation.

Part Four

RETURN TO THE ORDER OF FINITE BEINGS

CHAPTER I

THE WORLD OF CREATION

WE HAVE reached the high point of our metaphysical ascent. From this summit we can now retrace our path toward the world of creation, and in the light of the attributes of God give a priori proof that certain characteristics must belong to any created universe. This new process of deduction will allow us to meet up again with the theses proposed in our metaphysics of the finite, and even to add something to them. Our procedure here will be the counterpart of that employed in our initial investigation.

To avoid unnecessary repetition, we shall give only a brief outline.

§ 1. *The Perfect Initial Order*

Every creation forms a determined order of finite active substances which will include at least one personal being.

If God creates beings which are distinct from Himself, these creatures must be finite or limited participations of His Infinite Being. He cannot create an infinite being, another "Himself," since it is contradictory that there be several Infinites.[1] God can be participated in only by finite beings. For these to be finite they must be composed in the order of

1. See above, Part III, chap. II, § 2, n. 3.

subsistence (the constitutive composition of the finite).

Must these finite beings be active? What is the *raison d'être* of their activity? What profound significance does it have?

In God, existence, consciousness, enjoyment, and power are identified. This amounts to saying that the Absolute Being, source and exemplary cause of all being, is *essentially* consciousness, enjoyment, and power. Consequently, the finite world which is a participation of the Infinite, is necessarily a participation of the divine consciousness, enjoyment, and power. In other words, it must necessarily include one or several finite *persons* who are capable of intellectual consciousness, intellectual enjoyment, and a certain power or causality.

We could arrive at the same conclusion in another way. Indeed we have shown that a purely material world would be devoid of sense; hence God would not have a sufficient motive for creating it. The material world has no end in itself or value in itself, nor would it have any value for God either, since it would not bring Him any increase of perfection or enjoyment. If the created universe is to have an end, if it is to make sense, then it should include at least one spiritual or personal being who is capable of intellectual knowledge and intellectual enjoyment.

But can a finite being be consciousness, enjoyment, and power, in its very being and by its very being? St. Thomas believes that it cannot, and his studied opinion seems to be quite sound.[2] It may, however, be made more precise and complete.

If the created person had only to become conscious of himself and his complete dependence on God, and then enjoy this double knowledge, it is difficult to see why one single

2. *Summa Theologica,* I^a, qu. 54, art. 1-3; qu. 59, art. 2.

purely spiritual being could not carry out this twofold operation by its very being. It is doubtless true that the finite being is limited in its being, but to know himself fully he does not have to go beyond his own limits, except to seize the relation of radical dependence which binds him to the Infinite. But this relation is inscribed in his very being, and it would be sufficient then for the finite being to be fully conscious of himself to know that he was a creature.

The need for a second act or for accidental activity becomes clear in so far as we can show that a finite being cannot exist alone, but must be part of an order embracing two or more finite beings. This fact seems to be implied in the very nature of the finite being, and seems to be required also by the wisdom of God. It is quite true that the finite does not need other finites to be constituted in itself as a finite participation of the Infinite. It owes this to the composition of *esse* and *essentia*. But what sense would this *essentia* or principle of diversity have, if it were not opposed to other similar principles, to other essences or taleites? On the other hand, how could a finite being participate in the divine power and exercise any causality if it were the only existing creature? Hence, if the work of God is not to be constitutionally imperfect, if it is to be truly the expression of God's supreme perfection, there must be many varied finite beings which will express the infinite richness of their transcendent Cause by the harmonious co-operation of their different natures. In this way the unique and simple perfection of the Infinite finds a relatively perfect echo in an order of finite beings, embracing many composed beings which complete one another and yet are distinguished from each other.

But then the problem of activity immediately arises. Since he is a member of an order of finite beings, the created person would no longer develop his possibilities of knowing and enjoying to the fullest if he remained confined within his own limits. For now a complete self-knowledge requires that he see himself as part of the order of finite beings. To enjoy himself fully he must at the same time enjoy the whole order. The created person could not realize either of these by his very being, for this existence of itself is isolated and confined within its own limits. It is true that his existence relates him to everything which is, but this is only in a confused and merely virtual way. The finite being must then enter into relations with other finite beings, and in some way assimilate the reality which belongs to them.

Is such a thing possible, and in what way? Even though we have a certain knowledge of the attributes of God, this would hardly enable us to solve these questions in an a priori way. For our grasp of being is so inadequate that analysis of it alone would not reveal the possibility of secondary acts or accidental activity. To learn that, we must appeal to our own experience of ourselves as active, and show as we have already done above that every finite being is necessarily active. We must show that "to be" and "to be a principle of activity" signify one and the same thing for the finite substance. But once we have established this point, then the mystery of finite being suddenly clears away. For thanks to his activity, the created person can participate abundantly in the perfection of his Creator; his consciousness enlarges into a knowledge of the universal order; his enjoyment extends to the whole universe; finally, the causality which he exercises toward other finite beings makes him participate in the power of the Creator. This is the great vision of the created order in which every person, even though he be limited in his own being, can enrich himself infinitely by his transcendental activity, and thus imitate as far as possible the infinite perfection of his Author.

If God creates, then, He must create *several* finite beings. He must create at least two, since an isolated finite being could not realize its power of acting and of acquiring secondary perfections. In other words, he could not hope to exist as fully as his nature requires. It is by activity that the finite substance breaks out of its isolation by entering into relations with other finite substances and tries to win for itself, as far as it can, the perfection of the whole universe. If there were only one creature, this would be impossible. This one creature would be doomed to imperfection by the will of God Himself. But such a doom would be incompatible with the Creator's benevolence and wisdom.

What is the significance of the material world in this perspective? The beings which are inferior to man have no consciousness, enjoyment, personality, or end in themselves. They participate only very inadequately in the divine perfections. In them we do not find the *image* of the Creative Mind, but only a *vestige*.[3] What is knowledge in us becomes in them only biological assimilation or simple physical passivity. What is will in us becomes in them only a biological tendency or simple natural affinity. The personal influence that we exercise around ourselves becomes in them only a transitive and fixed action on their immediate environment. It is true that animals, plants, and non-living bodies possess in different degrees the characteristics of individuality (unity and autonomy), and that they are therefore true active substances. But their activity is entirely conditioned by extension. It is never perfectly immanent even in the case of living organisms. It is a transitive action, exercised only within a limited radius and never surpassing the corporeal

3. See above, Part III, chap. III, § 3, footnote 9.

world. What significance can this inferior activity, whether biological or physical, have?

As we have already said, the beings which are inferior to man have meaning only when taken in a human context, when they are considered as continuations of man and as conditions for his earthly existence. It is the task of special metaphysics to determine the role and the anthropocentric value of the material universe, and of the different categories of beings which are found in it.

The collection of created substances forms a limited collection, not an infinite collection. For in fact, everything which exists is distinct or determined, and the determination proper to a collection or multitude is finiteness, that is, the possibility of numbering or counting its units.

These created substances form an order, not merely a *static* order as we have already seen, but a *dynamic* order, one which is necessarily made up of natures which complement one another and are intended to perfect one another by their mutual activity. Each of them finds the needed complement for its power of acting in the order of finite substances. This new light on the question of the order of finite beings is a reflection from our considerations on the wisdom and benevolence of God. Since the created world is produced by an act of wisdom and love, and since its purpose is to participate in the goodness and happiness of God, it is impossible that this world should be *essentially* imperfect or incomplete. It is impossible that there should be some created substances which could not reach their secondary perfection because of a defect inherent in the very constitution of the created order. Hence, it is impossible that a finite substance should need oxygen to breathe, and yet that oxygen would not be provided in the divine plan. For this would be an essential disorder which would be charge-able to the First Cause itself.

The creative act has as its term or effect an order of finite active substances. The immediate result of the divine voli-tion is that finite substances exist, and that they are principles of an activity proportionate to their nature. Traditional philosophy believed that in the divine causality we must dis-tinguish *creation, conservation,* and *motion.* In other words, God would give existence; He would conserve creatures in existence; and He would move them in their activity. This view held that God must intervene again to enable the cre-ated substance to go beyond itself and produce its secondary acts. Such dissection of the creative act and its immediate effect made it extremely difficult to explain how God moves things. It implies that the First Cause intervened not only at the *beginning* of the activity, but even in the secondary act itself, either under the form of the "physical premotion" of Bannez, or under the guise of the "simultaneous co-op-eration" of Molina. But in both these views it is difficult to see how the creature can still be free.

As a matter of fact there is no reason for saying that God intervenes in several different ways. Nor is there any reason for speaking about several terms of this causality, which would really succeed one another or be really distinguishable from one another; thus, for example, to exist, to continue to exist, to act. In fact, to create means to will that something exist; it means to give existence, and to give existence is to give everything. On the part of God, creation is one single continuing influx. On the part of the effect, there is the same unity and the same permanence, but "participated" and therefore imperfect. The effect which God produces is *unique,* that is, the order of finite substances realizing a unity which is both static and dynamic. The effect of God is *permanent,* but it is a permanence which implies an unceasing dynamism. To be, to endure, and to be active, are one and the same thing for finite substances, and it is this which is the immediate effect of the creative act. In other words, under the continuing action of God the order of substances exists, perdures, and is the principle of unceasing activities which determine the evolution and growth of the entire order. This evolution can even include substantial changes, if there are substances which are determinable in their very essence.[4]

Scholastics have speculated on whether God could create several worlds which would be completely independent of each other. We can state that everything which exists and is the effect of God will form one single *static* order because of the ontological similarity uniting all beings. As far as determining whether all creatures form one and the same *dynamic* order, whether they are all united among themselves by their activities, this is not so clear, even though the divine attributes of simplicity and wisdom seem to argue in favor of the perfect unity of God's work.

Let us note that a better understanding of this one continuing creative influx helps us solve certain particularly difficult problems concerning creative causality. Thus we need a proper appreciation of the creative act and its immediate effect (the perduring order of finite active substances) to understand how the evolution of the world can produce substances by substantial change; how human souls are created at the term of a biological process of conception; the increase of being which is implied in all the activity of the finite being; finally, the genuine liberty of the created person who is capable of determining the direction of his own voluntary activity for himself.

4. See above, Part II, chap. II, § 4, footnote 2; and chap. III, § 2, n. 2.

§ 2. The Final Order and the Evolution of the Universe

This perfect initial order tends to a final order by a determined process of evolution.

We have said that the created order is necessarily *perfect* in the sense that it cannot involve any essential disorder or any essential defect. However, this order still strives toward further perfection because all the finite substances composing it are essentially dynamic. The created world is constantly developing its inherent potentialities. It perfects itself more and more through the activity of the finite beings. For this reason we can distinguish between the initial order, or the starting point of the universal process of evolution, and the final order to which the process tends.

But does this process of evolution really tend toward a *term,* toward a lasting and permanent state? Is not the evolution of the universe endless? Can it not be such? Here we must recall that personal beings are the really essential elements in the universe. The material world exists only for persons; its destiny is subordinate to theirs. Every person has a value in himself, an end proper to himself, a destiny which he must reach. God's wisdom and benevolence seem to require that persons should be able to reach a state of lasting perfection and definitive happiness. It is quite true that this final state or last end does not exclude all new activity and accidental progress. But it must exclude any moral insecurity and possible loss of happiness.

In this sense the evolution of the created universe toward its last end is *determined*. However, this statement will not stand without qualification.

First of all, the process of evolution has a determined *starting point* and, consequently, a determined *duration*. For in point of fact, the order of finite substances was nec-

essarily created in a determined state. The evolution of the
world takes place within that framework. The successive
phases of this evolution are therefore numerable or meas-
urable. They had a first term, and the series of these successive states is and always will be a finite or determined
series with unlimited growth.

These views differ considerably from those which St.
Thomas, under the influence of pagan philosophy, held on
this same point. The principles to which we appeal in our
rejection of a quantitative infinite were formulated clearly by
St. Thomas,[5] but when examining the question of the duration of the material world, he was impressed by the fact that
all the pagan philosophers since Aristotle had held that matter and the cosmos were eternal. St. Thomas was discon-
certed by this unanimous consent. Indiscreet men like Siger
of Brabant had thrown considerable suspicion on Aristotle's
teaching. St. Thomas saw that the Philosopher's views required careful handling. On this point, then, he adopted a
position midway between the views of the conservative
theologians and those of the radical Aristotelians. Against
the pagans, he held that the eternity of the world was not
evident; but he also held, against the theologians, that we
cannot show its impossibility, and that Revelation alone can
guarantee that the world had a beginning.

St. Thomas had ample justification for separating the
problem of creation from that of the duration of the corporeal world. It is not properly because the world is created
that it has a limited temporal duration. *Factum ex nihilo*
does not mean *factum post nihilum,* as St. Bonaventure
thought. On the contrary, as long as we limit ourselves to
the immediate effect of the creative act, that is, to the *order
of finite substances,* it is pointless to ask about the beginning

5. *Summa Theologica,* I⁰, qu. 7, art. 4.

or end of this order. Since the Cause of this order is eternal, with respect to what could the order have "begun" to be? Certainly not with respect to God, since the divine duration is not successive; and certainly not with respect to anything else, since nothing else exists. From this same point of view it is meaningless to talk about the "end" of this substantial order. We cannot describe the duration which the order of created substances has in terms of "before" and "after."

Yet these substances are active, and every activity implies becoming, evolution, growth, and hence successive duration; and where the material world is concerned, activity implies a successive continued duration, that is, a temporal duration. It is from this point of view that we can speak of a beginning and an end. Did the evolution of the corporeal world have a beginning? should it have had a beginning? must it have an end?

It must have had a *beginning;* otherwise it would be completely indeterminate, and consequently unthinkable and impossible. For every existent thing is distinct or determined. The process of evolution of the material universe is an actuality and, in so far as the past is concerned, it is already completed. It is therefore determined. The determination proper to a series is its finiteness or its capacity of being numbered. Consequently, the series of past events is finite. It had a first term, and time had a beginning.

Furthermore, the hypothesis of an evolution without a starting point involves a contradiction. This contradiction has been often demonstrated. A typical *reductio ad absurdum* follows. If the time past were eternal and if, as Aristotle thought, the revolutions of the stars were eternal, then an infinity of days would have elapsed up to the present time. In that case we would have to say that any "past" day lies at a finite distance from today, and consequently that no one of them is infinitely removed. But then the past is finite, because there would be a day located at a finite distance from today which would yet be the furthest away of all, and consequently the first day. Or we would have to say that one or several days of the past are at an infinite distance from today. How then can we conceive the passage from the days which are infinitely removed to the days which are located at a finite distance from us? This leaves us in complete confusion.

Will the evolution of the created world come to an end? This question can be understood in two different ways. First, it might mean that the created universe, once arrived at a certain phase of its evolution, would *cease to exist*. This is the hypothesis of the annihilation of creation. Some think the hypothesis absurd, because it would involve two successive decrees in God, one opposed to the other: first that of creating, and then that of stopping His creative influx. This would mean God had altered His decree. But this argument does not seem convincing, for immutability only excludes becoming in the strict sense, the becoming which involves dependence. It does not exclude the sovereign acts of divine liberty. It seems possible then that God could will that the universe exist for a determined period until its evolution was complete. However, any such annihilation of creation seems to be ruled out by the wisdom and benevolence of God. For if God bestows existence on *persons* who have a value in themselves, who aspire to a definitive happiness, and who are by nature capable of a lasting final end, then the annihilation of these persons can hardly be reconciled with the Creator's wisdom and love.

But the "end of the world" and the "end of time" can be understood in yet another sense: the universe, having arrived at a certain stage of its evolution, might reach a state of

stable perfection and stop evolving. We have noted the
sense in which the created order must apparently arrive at a
final state, where all the created persons will have reached
the goal of their essential perfection. However, the final
state does not exclude all successive activity, because of the
very nature of activity. We must then allow for the idea of
an unlimited duration in the future, or the idea of an
"eternal" successive duration in the future. A concept of
this kind does not entail any of the inconveniences involved
in the notion of an eternity in the past; the past is already
accomplished, and therefore an eternal past would mean the
realization of an infinite series of events or an *infinite in
act*. Eternity in the future supposes an *infinite in potency,*
that is, a series which is always finite, but is of unlimited
growth. This concept does not involve any difficulty.

Can we establish any relation between the duration of the
created universe and the divine eternity? Everything which
exists, coexists with God. Hence at any moment of time we
can truthfully say, "God is." These two durations are simultaneous, but this is an *inadequate* simultaneity, for the divine
eternity is not successive and is not measured by the beginning of temporal duration. Consequently, God and the
world are "simultaneous," but they are not "contemporary."
Only two "temporal" events can be "contemporary."

We have just seen how the evolution of the created universe must be determined in duration. Further, it must also
have a determined *orientation*. Here again a distinction must
be made. In so far as the evolution of the universe results
from the essential tendencies of created natures, it is completely determined by the First Cause who creates the order
of natures. But in so far as the evolution of this universe is
due to free agents, they can determine the direction of that
evolution by their own free decisions. Every free act which

expresses itself by impact on the material world, has indefinite repercussions on the future evolution of the world. Think, for example, of the incalculable consequences of the free act by which I kill some insect or pull up a weed. Think of the incomparably more formidable consequences of a free decision which plunges peoples into war or keeps them at peace.

§ 3. The Problem of Evil

The created order, which is perfect as an order, may contain imperfect elements. Here we are face to face with the problem of evil, which has always tormented men's minds, and which still remains the principal objection of the atheists. It is the function of the metaphysician to lay bare the profound ontological roots of evil, and to formulate the fundamental laws which govern the solution of the problem.

The possibility or necessity of evil cannot be proved in any purely a priori way by analysis of the ideas of creation and of finite participation in the Infinite. Evil is the privation of a good, or a disorder in the activity of a being. Why should this privation or disorder be necessary, or even possible, in the effects of divine wisdom and benevolence? Yet the existence of evil is a *fact,* a datum of our experience; there is disorder in the universe, and beings do lack the perfection required by their nature. We must try now to determine the origin, nature, and significance of the fact of evil.

We have seen that every being is good or desirable in so far as being. A being cannot be evil in so far as it exists. Evil therefore is not "a being." Every being is the principle of an activity proportionate to its nature, an activity which tends to realize as far as possible the secondary perfection of the subject. It is in activity, and only in activity, that there can be any question of imperfection, deviation, or disorder, to the extent to which this activity contradicts the agent's basic nature. How is such a thing possible? The answer cannot be *a priori;* it must be derived from experience.

Physical evil is possible in the case of the activity of corporeal beings. The activity of bodies is transitive and always mixed with passivity. It can run counter to the activity of other bodies; thus harmony is not always had between these competing activities. *Moral* evil is possible in the case of man's spiritual activity. His free activity may reveal a deliberate and culpable deviation from the moral law. These facts show that physical and moral evil are connected with the nature of created things, and are therefore necessarily possible. In the hypothesis that God creates an order of corporeal substances, and of human substances which are partially spiritual, physical evil and moral evil are unavoidable.[6]

Physical evil does not constitute a serious difficulty as long as we consider only the material world. The beings which make up that world have no proper end or value in themselves. They exist only for the sake of mankind. But in the evolution of the material world physical evil is an integral and even an essential element. Conflict among corporeal beings is not only inevitable, but actually contributes to the harmonious evolution of the universe by periodically eliminating those surplus creatures which threaten to make the earth uninhabitable. The "suffering" of animals would raise a problem if it were proven that this was suffering in the strict sense, that is, *conscious* suffering. But conscious-

6. I am purposely not considering the hypothesis of a creation of purely spiritual substances, because it is not certain that an angel can sin in the natural order. Nor do we have to inquire to what extent a preternatural or supernatural intervention of God could eliminate the possibility of physical or moral evil.

ness supposes spirituality, and animals give no evidence of spirituality.

Physical evil causes a problem when it afflicts man, and it reveals itself as physical or moral suffering. But suffering which is accepted can be a means of instructing, developing, elevating, strengthening, and perfecting man's whole personality. The supreme physical evil of death serves to free man from his uncertain condition here below and opens the door to that enduring state which is the goal of his spiritual nature.

From this point of view, the physical evils affecting man while he is part of the world evolution, become a means of achieving his destiny, a means which does not endanger the final order of creation.[7]

Moral evil involves more difficulty, because this evil affects the person who has a value in himself. If this evil is definitive, if the unruly human will persists in its disorder, then the final order of creation involves a definitive and irreparable disorder. Here we are confronted with the fact of human liberty and its terrifying possibilities. Men determine their own fate by the way they use this noble power. They are indeed called to increasing love of the good and observance of the moral law, but they can still abuse their free will. However, they will be held responsible for such

7. These few remarks do not pretend to exhaust the problem of human suffering. On the contrary, I believe that in human life this problem presents a great many moral aspects which cannot be adequately solved without taking into account the order of grace and redemption. When examining these problems, however, we must guard against being mislead by our own feelings and impressions. Thus the problem of death is no more tragic when 50,000 people perish in a few moments in an earthquake than it is when one single person succumbs to cancer after years of suffering. The problem of death is no more agonizing when 50,000 people die in a bombed city than it is when on the same day the same number of people die from different diseases or accidents in various parts of the world.

abuse and must face the consequences of it. What are these consequences? Does moral evil or sin involve by its very nature an immanent sanction? Does this sanction affect the unrepentant sinner in a future life? Is the moral attitude held in one's last hour fixed immutably by death? Philosophy can only guess at the answers. God's wisdom and benevolence suggest the following reply.

God created the world out of pure benevolence to allow created persons to participate in His own goodness and happiness. Observance of the moral law is the necessary condition for man's moral goodness; respect for the moral law is also essential for man's happiness. In God's creation moral disorder entails loss of happiness, a sanction which is made definitive by death.

Would it be possible for all created persons to persist obstinately in their disorder and thus miss their final end? In that case would not creation be a complete failure? Here again philosophy can give no answer. In the purely natural order, man without grace would be thrown completely on his own resources and thus every man could, at least in theory, abuse his freedom. Even that reverse would in no way affect the Creative Cause; first, because the reponsibility for moral evil falls entirely upon the guilty creature; secondly, even in its misfortune the creature must still bear witness to the wisdom, benevolence, justice, and holiness of God.

Chapter II

CONCLUSION

§ 1. The Results of Our Inquiry

ONTOLOGY investigates what the affirmation of being really implies when being is understood not merely as a brute fact, or as object of experience, but as a basic intelligible value. The results of this investigation are of capital importance.

In every existent reality the intelligence discovers a transcendental value by virtue of which this reality belongs to the *universal community of beings*. These beings constitute one single order, a universe, all the elements of which are bound together by a basic ontological similarity. From the fact that something exists we can infer that something exists by itself, and therefore exists necessarily. This necessary reality we have called the *absolute*. On the other hand, the fact of the multiple and the fact of becoming (simultaneous diversity and successive diversity) pose the metaphysical problem of the finite being and the antinomy of the *absolute and the finite*. This antinomy is solved by the affirmation of the Infinite Being, the affirmation of a Being which transcends the order of finite beings. The derivation of the attributes of this Infinite Being throws new light on the relation between the finite and the Infinite and on the nature of the created world.

In short, ontology is only the scientific, the systematic, and critical exposition of the reasoning which raises man from the consciousness of himself to the affirmation of his God.

§ 2. The Method of Ontology

We can now describe the method of ontology somewhat more precisely. This method is not simple, nor purely empirical, nor purely deductive, nor properly inductive. It contains the following elements.

1. *An Empirical Method.*—By an appeal to experience we see that something exists. We become conscious of our own thinking and willing which show that all reality is intelligible and desirable. We see that the real is diversified and that it changes. We become aware of certain distinctive characteristics of the self (unity, autonomy, evolution, and so forth) and in particular of its activity.

2. *An Analytical Method.*—This method is applied in our analysis of the content of experience, of the concept of being, of the multiple, of change, and of activity.

3. *A Deductive Method.*—The passage from implicit to explicit knowledge is developed in the deduction of the transcendental attributes; in the metaphysical inferences (the constitutive compositions, the relativity of the finite in its existence, the composition of potency and act, the relativity of change, the composition from substance and power of operation, the relativity of the active subject, the existence of the Infinite); in showing that activity is a property of every finite being; in the deduction of the attributes of the Infinite; in deducing the essential characteristics of the created order.

4. *A Transcendentalising Method.*—This critical reflection on the profound meaning of the idea of being is the distinctive characteristic of true metaphysical research. It allows us to discover the transcendental extension of this idea and the transcendental capacity of the intelligence. This method enables metaphysical thought to surpass all

forms of empiricism, particularly Kantian phenomenalism and agnosticism, and to reach the level of the transcendental and the absolute.

§ 3. Accretions to be Eliminated

Our treatise has tried to pay particular attention to method, precision, and critical accuracy. We said above that scholastics must prove that Thomistic philosophy can meet all the requirements for truly systematic and critical thought, and that its precision equals or surpasses the exactness of history's most brilliant metaphysical syntheses. For this reason we must firmly exclude from ontology every problem which does not have a strict bearing on the object of metaphysics. Accordingly, we believe that the following subject matter should be eliminated from a treatise on ontology.

1. *The Armory of Definitions.*—Ordinarily, too many definitions encumber the study of the transcendental attributes. Such often are the definitions of the derived senses of the notions of unity, truth, and goodness; of the notions related to these transcendental concepts, or to their derivatives; and of the classification of all possible kinds of distinctions and compositions. Either we find that these abstract definitions are given somewhat arbitrarily, or we are forced to anticipate later topics in a way which interrupts the natural progress of our metaphysical investigation.

2. *The Dynamism Proper to the Corporeal World.*—The object of ontology or general metaphysics is to study the laws common to every being as being; this includes the primary "division" of being into finite beings and Infinite Being. The relation of the finite to the Infinite is essential for any understanding of the ontological order. The study of the laws proper to the classes of finite beings which we

can distinguish, in the world of experience (man, non-conscious living things, and non-living matter) belongs properly to special metaphysics (anthropology, biology, cosmology). Consequently, it is the province of special metaphysics to study extension and the continuous, transitive action, substantial becoming, and the hylomorphic composition.

3. *The Aristotelian Classification of the Categories or the Predicaments.*—Aristotle's classification of the categories results from an analysis or "division" of the "First Substance." This analysis leads the Philosopher to distinguish substance, properly speaking, and nine [1] categories of accidents: quality, quantity, relation, time, place, action, passion, habitus, and situation. This empirical classification is quite superficial. Furthermore, most of these categories apply only to the corporeal world; such, for example, are quantity, time, place, action, passion, habitus, and situation. These belong, therefore, to special metaphysics. Only three categories belong in ontology: substance, quality, and relation. Now the study of these categories can, in fact, be reduced to the study of the activity of finite beings. This is quite clear in the case of substance; quality, or the accidental determination, is merely the second act determining the substance's power of operation; and the predicamental relation results from the activity which puts a finite thing in "relation" with other finite beings.

In traditional treatises on ontology, considerable space is devoted to relations. Authors distinguish *transcendental* relation and *predicamental* relation. The first exists between two components or two principles of being; the second unites two subsistent beings. The scholastics asked whether there

1. We can omit here the exegetical problem concerning the exact number of the Aristotelian categories. The scholastic tradition generally holds that there are ten categories.

were *real* predicamental relations, that is, relations which would constitute *real accidents,* distinct from the two related subjects. Such entities however are superfluous. The relation as such is an abstraction, the work of the intelligence. It is real when it rests upon real foundations. Thus the relation of filiation between a son and his father is real, because this son was actually begotten by this father. It is based upon a real biological activity, of which the father is the principle and the son is the result.

We do not have to make relation the object of a special study in ontology. For relation is constantly intruding all through our metaphysical investigation. Thus, for example, are the relations which define the attributes of being; the correlation between the components of finite being; the relation of dependence of finite being in its existence, its becoming, and its activity. Our gradual and progressive discovery of the network of relations which make the universe intelligible finally reveals to us the *metaphysical order,* that static and dynamic order of finite beings which subsist in total dependence on the Infinite.

4. *The Problem of Subsistence or Personality.*—It is quite obvious that the impact of theology led to the introduction of this problem into metaphysics. The aim was to prepare a satisfactory explanation for the mystery of the Incarnation. It is a question of knowing how and why the human nature of Jesus Christ does not constitute a human *person.* But this problem is extraneous to philosophy and must remain so. For from the metaphysical point of view, there is no reason for distinguishing between the *individual nature* and the *individual* (person).

5. *The Aristotelian Theory of Causes.*—Like the classification of the categories, this theory rests upon an empirical analysis of causality in the physical world. Most of it per-

tains to special metaphysics (treatment of constitutive causes, material and formal; motive cause; the finality of movement in the corporeal world). In a strict sense only the metaphysical principle of efficient causality, the notion of finality in the activity of finite beings, and the notion of creative cause (efficient, exemplary, and final), should be treated in ontology according as the natural development of the investigation may require.

§ 4. The Love of the True

Differences in temperament, education, personal interests, and conviction will cause men to react very differently to the same work of philosophy. Consequently, the present book, based upon a clearly defined theory of knowledge and following the principles of metaphysical realism and rigorous intellectualism, can hardly fail to be a "sign of contradiction."

Readers accustomed to the classical manuals of Thomistic ontology will find that this treatise often proposes new views which may seem somewhat strange and perhaps somewhat daring. They will reproach the author for abandoning traditional views and may even charge him with seeking novelty at any cost in a field where truth has long since been acquired. Others may find this treatise deplorably "scholastic," and they will be astonished to find that it still retains certain Thomistic doctrines which they believed definitely out-moded by modern criticism.

Still others may appreciate the author's constant care to keep in touch with reality and to build a genuine science of the existent as existent, avoiding the "notionalism," "logicism," and "rationalism" still too prevalent even in our best scholastic manuals. The devotees of existentialism and supporters of the positive sciences may consider our metaphysics only an empty juggling of abstractions and principles, the fruit of an emaciated intellectualism which has lost contact with the concrete reality.

Our completely systematic exposition of ontology will, however, appeal to some who may appreciate the care we have taken to *demonstrate* rather than merely to *affirm;* our concern to trace the logical sequence of thought, and our insistence on clarity rather than elegance in expression. And yet we are aware that these "scholastic" demonstrations will be irritating to many for whom the syllogism can only be an insufferable annoyance.

We would be indeed naïve to think that everyone will accept our view of ontology. But we can at least ask those interested in metaphysical problems to examine impartially the method to be used in this field. Can man get beyond empiricism to the transcendent by any other means than conceptual and discursive thought? The so-called "existentialist" methods are doubtless of great use in exploring the various aspects of our own lived experience. But they appear completely unsuited for giving us those conditions of existence common to all finite beings, which we must grasp to be able to affirm the existence of the Infinite.

Ontology is a stern, exacting discipline. Imagination, emotion, or sentiment have no place in it. It demands a continual asceticism in thought. Metaphysical inference gives only improper and analogical knowledge. Our minds find that knowledge hard to handle. Aristotle had already noted that when dealing with the supreme truths man's mind is somewhat like the owl, blinded by the excessive glare of the sun. Yet, however weak the intellectual vision of metaphysics may be, it is still the supreme achievement of man's intellect, and a mind fired by the love of truth will gladly exchange the easy knowledge of earthly things for a single feeble ray of the Eternal Truth.

BIBLIOGRAPHY

WE HAVE deliberately limited this bibliography to the texts of St. Thomas and to works inspired by Thomism. We believe that eclectic introductions which claim to broaden the student's point of view only succeed in making it more difficult for him to accustom himself to philosophical thinking. Our aim, therefore, has been to provide a list of works which, though selective, are sufficiently varied in their presentation of the problems of ontology to stimulate the reader to further personal reflection. Finally, the more advanced student will find in the works here listed additional bibliographical material relative to modern philosophy.

The Principal Texts of Saint Thomas

De ente et essentia (1254-1256). This famous opusculum, belonging to the youth of St. Thomas, is difficult and baffling reading for beginners. The student might profitably consult the text and commentary prepared by M. D. Roland-Gos‧ selin: *Le "De Ente et Essentia" De S. Thomas (Bibliothèque Thomiste, VIII)*, Kain: Le Saulchoir, 1926.

Summa contra Gentiles (1259-1264). The first three books contain the earliest synthetic exposition of St. Thomas' philosophical ideas, which he here opposes to those of the pagan philosophers.

Quaestiones disputatae de potentia Dei (1265-1268?). This tract contains an important series of questions on the power and simplicity of God, creation, and the conservation of creatures.

Summa theologica (1266-1273). St. Thomas' masterpiece, noted for its clarity and conciseness. See especially *De Deo* (qu. 2-26); *De processione creaturarum a Deo* (qu. 44-49); *De gubernatione rerum a Deo* (qu. 103-119).

In metaphysicam Aristotelis commentaria (1266-1272). Though this work contains many interesting expositions, St. Thomas' thought is restricted in large measure by the text upon which he is commenting.

Works on Thomistic Ontology

WORKS IN ENGLISH

Adler, M. "The Demonstration of God's Existence," *The Thomist,* V (January, 1943), pp. 182-218.

Anderson, J. F. *The Bond of Being.* St. Louis: Herder, 1949.

Bastable, P. K. *Desire for God.* London and Dublin: Burns, Oates & Washbourne, Ltd., 1947.

Bourke, V. J. "Experience of Extra-Mental Reality as the Starting Point of St. Thomas' Metaphysics," *Proc. Amer. Cath. Phil. Assn.,* XIV (1938), pp. 135-41.

Brosnan, W., S.J. *God and Reason.* New York: Fordham Univ. Press, 1924.

————. *God Infinite and Reason.* New York: America Press, 1928.

Bryar, W. *St. Thomas and the Existence of God: Three Interpretations.* Chicago: H. Regnery, 1951.

————. "Adler and the Existence of God," *The New Scholasticism,* XVIII (July, 1944), pp. 270-83.

Carpenter, H., O.P. "The Historical Aspects of the Quinque Viae," *God.* Ed. C. Lattey, S.J. London: Sheed & Ward, 1931, pp. 196-216.

————. "The Philosophical Approach to God in Thomism." *The Thomist,* I (April, 1939), pp. 45-61.

Coffey, P. *Ontology.* New York: Smith, 1938.

Collins, J. *The Thomistic Philosophy of the Angels.* Washington: Catholic Univ. Press, 1947.

D'Arcy, M. C., S.J. *The Pain of this World and the Province of God.* London: Longmans, Green & Co., 1935.

Donovan, Sr. M. Annice. *The Henological Argument for the Existence of God in the Works of St. Thomas Aquinas.* Doctoral dissertation, University of Notre Dame, 1946.

Donnelly, P. J., S.J. "Gratuity of the Beatific Vision and the Possibility of a Natural Destiny," *Theological Studies,* XI (September, 1950), pp. 374-404.

Farrell, W. *A Companion to the Summa.* New York: Sheed & Ward, 1938-1942.

Garrigou-Lagrange, R., O.P. *God, His Existence and His Nature.* Trans. Dom Bede Rose, O.S.B. St. Louis: Herder, 1934-1936.

Gilson, E. *The Spirit of Medieval Philosophy.* Trans. A. H. C. Downes. New York: Scribners, 1940.

————. *God and Philosophy.* New Haven: Yale Univ. Press, 1941.

————. *The Philosophy of St. Thomas Aquinas.* Trans. E. Bullough. St. Louis: Herder, 1941.

————. *Being and Some Philosophers.* Trans. A. H. C. Downes. Toronto: Pontifical Institute of Medieval Studies, 1949.

Hawkins, D. *Causality and Implication.* New York: Sheed & Ward, 1937.

Hesburgh, T. *God and the World of Man.* South Bend, Ind.: Univ. of Notre Dame Press, 1950.

Joyce, G., S.J. *Principles of Natural Theology.* New York: Longmans, 1923.

Knox, Ronald. *God and the Atom.* London: Sheed & Ward, 1945.

McCormick, J., S.J. *Scholastic Metaphysics.* Chicago: Loyola Univ. Press, 1928.

Maritain, J. *A Preface to Metaphysics.* Trans. E. I. Watkin. New York: Sheed & Ward, 1939.

————. *St. Thomas and the Problem of Evil.* Milwaukee: Marquette Univ. Press, 1942.

————. *Existence and the Existent.* Trans. L. Galantière and G. B. Phelan. New York: Pantheon Books, 1949.

Meehan, F. X. *Efficient Causality in Aristotle and in St. Thomas.* Doctoral dissertation. Catholic University, 1940.

O'Connor, W. *The Natural Desire for God.* Milwaukee: Marquette Univ. Press, 1948.

O'Mahoney, J. E. *The Desire of God in the Philosophy of St. Thomas Aquinas.* London: Longmans, 1929.

Osgniach, A. *Analysis of Objects*. New York: Wagner, 1938.

Owens, J., C.SS.R. "Theodicy, Natural Theology, and Metaphysics," *The Modern Schoolman*, XXVIII (January, 1951), pp. 126-37.

Pace, E. A. "The Teleology of St. Thomas," *The New Scholasticism*, I (July, 1927), pp. 213-31.

Pegis, A. C. "Molina and Human Liberty," *Jesuit Thinkers of the Renaissance*. Milwaukee: Marquette Univ. Press, 1939, pp. 75-131.

————. "The Dilemma of Being and Unity," *Essays in Thomism*. New York: Sheed & Ward, 1942, pp. 151-83; 379-82.

————. "Between Thought and Being," *Thought*, XX (September, 1945), pp. 473-98.

Phelan, G. B. *St. Thomas and Analogy*. Milwaukee: Marquette Univ. Press, 1941.

Phillips, P. R. *Modern Thomistic Philosophy*. London: Burns, Oates & Washbourne, Ltd., 1934-1935. (New ed. 1939-1940.)

Pontifex, R., O.S.B. *The Existence of God*. London: Longmans, Green & Co., 1946.

Renard, H., S.J. *The Philosophy of Being*. Milwaukee: Bruce, 1943.

————. *The Philosophy of God*. Milwaukee: Bruce, 1951.

Rickaby, J., S.J. *Of God and His Creatures*. Westminster, Md.: The Carroll Press, 1950.

Schumacher, M., C.S.C. *The Knowableness of God, its Relation to the Theory of Knowledge in St. Thomas*. Doctoral dissertation, University of Notre Dame, 1905.

Schwartz, H. T., T.O.P. "A Reply: The Demonstration of God's Existence," *The Thomist*, VI (April, 1943), pp. 19-49.

Sheen, F. J. *Philosophy of Religion*. New York: Appleton-Century-Crofts, 1948.

————. *God and Intelligence in Modern Philosophy. A Critical Study in the Light of the Philosophy of St. Thomas Aquinas*. London. Longmans, 1925.

Smith, G., S.J. *Natural Theology*. New York: Macmillan, 1951.

Smith, G., S.J. "Before You Start Talking About God," *The Modern Schoolman*, XXII (November, 1945), pp. 24-43.

Smith, V. E. "On the Being of Metaphysics," *The New Scholasticism*, XX (January, 1946), pp. 72-84.

WORKS IN FRENCH

Balthasar, N. *L'être et les principes métaphysiques*. Louvain: 1914. A series of penetrating studies on the principal problems of metaphysics.

————. *La méthode en métaphysique*. Louvain: 1943. An original study of the basic problem of metaphysics and of the method which should be followed in solving it—"addressed to minds which have been matured by philosophical reflection."

Forest, A. *La structure métaphysique du concret selon saint Thomas d'Aquin*. Paris: 1931. A profound historical study of the great metaphysical doctrines of St. Thomas.

————. *Du consentement à l'être*. Paris: 1936. A Thomistic criticism of idealism, difficult for beginners.

Garrigou-Lagrange, R. *Dieu. Son existence et sa nature*. 6th ed.; Paris: 1933. A Thomistic solution of certain agnostic antinomies.

Grégoire, A. *Immanence et transcendance. Questions de théodicée*. Brussels-Paris: 1939. The influence of Father Maréchal is often noticeable in this clear and critical exposition of such subjects as the existence of God, the divine attributes, God and the World.

Maritain, J. *Sept leçons sur l'être et les premiers principes de la raison spéculative*. Paris: 1934. A penetrating examination of the fundamental problems of metaphysics.

Mercier, D. *Métaphysique générale ou Ontologie*. 1st ed.: Louvain: 1894: 7th ed., 1923. An interesting indication of the mentality prevalent at the end of the 19th century, in the heydey of positivism and scientism, this study reveals Cardinal Mercier's metaphysics as the most vulnerable part of his philosophical work.

De Raeymaker, L. *Philosophie de l'être. Essai de synthèse métaphysique*. Louvain: 1946. The author's completion of a series of exiellent studies published in Latin and in Dutch.

Metaphysica generalis, 1931; 2nd ed., 1935; *Ontologie. Algemeene Metaphysica,* 1933; *Metaphysiek van het zijn,* 1944.

Van Steenberghen, F. "La Composition constitutive de l'être fini," *Revue neoscolastique de philosophie,* XL (1938), pp. 489-518.

————. "Le Problems Philosophique de l'existence de Dieu," *Revue Philosophique de Louvain,* XLV (February, 1947), pp. 5-20; (May-August, 1947); pp. 141-168; (November, 1947), pp. 301-13.

————. "Precisions sur l'objet et la methode de l'ontologie," *Collectanea Mechliniensia* (Mechliniae), XXXII (1947), pp. 291-96.

————. "La physique moderne et l'existence de Dieu," *Revue Philosophique de Louvain,* XLVI (August, 1948), pp. 376-89.

Valensin, A. *A travers la métaphysique.* Paris: 1925. Remarkable studies of Kantianism, pantheism, analogy, and other problems related to the science of being.

Webert, J. *Essai de métaphysique thomiste.* Paris: 1927. A graceful presentation of the subject for educated laymen.

WORKS IN LATIN

Arnou, R., S.J. *Metaphysica Generalis.* Romae: Pont. Univ. Greg., 1941.

————. *Theologia Naturalis.* Romae: Pont. Univ. Greg., 1943.

————. *De quinque viis sancti Thomae ad demonstrandam Dei existentiam apud antiquos Graecos et Judaeos praeformatis vel adumbratis.* Romae: Pont. Univ. Greg. 1932.

Boyer, C., S.J. *Cursus Philosophiae.* Paris: Desclee de Brouwer, 1937.

Brosnan, W., S.J. *Institutiones Theologiae Naturalis.* Chicago: Loyola Univ. Press, 1921.

Davila, J. *Metaphysica Generalis.* Mexico City: Editorial Buena Prensa, 1946.

Del Prado, N., O.P. *De Veritate Fundamentali Philosophiae Christianae.* Friburgi Helvetiorum: Typis Consoc. S. Pauli, 1911.

Dezza, P., S.J. *Metaphysica Generalis,* Romae: Pont. Univ. Greg., 1948.

Esser, G., S.J. *Metaphysica Generalis.* Techny, Ill.: Mission
    Press, 1949.

——. *Theologia Naturalis.* Techny, Ill.: Mission Press, 1949.

Gisquière, E. *Deus Dominus. Praelectiones Theodiceae.* Paris:
    Beauchesne, 1950.

Gredt, J., O.S.B. *Elementa philosophiae aristotelico-thomis-
    ticae.* 10th ed., Freiburg: Herder, 1937.

Hontheim, J., S.J. *Theodicea sive Theologia Naturalis.* Frei-
    burg: Herder, 1926.

Mandato, P., S.J. *Institutiones philosophicae secundum doc-
    trinam Aristotelis et S.Th. Aq.* Romae: De Propag. Fide,
    1894.

Maquart, F. X. *Elementa philosophiae.* Paris: Blot, 1938.

De Raeymaker, L. *Metaphysica Generalis.* Louvain: Warny,
    1931; 2nd ed., 1935.

Rast, M. *Theologia Naturalis.* Freiburg: Herder, 1939.

Reinstadler, S. *Elementa philosophiae scholasticae.* 15th ed.,
    Freiburg: Herder, 1920.

Remer, V., S.J. *Theologia Naturalis.* 9th ed., cura P. Geny,
    S.J. Romae: Pont. Univ. Greg., 1947.

——. *Ontologia.* 8th ed., cura P. Geny, S.J. Romae: Pont.
    Univ. Greg., 1936.

TOPICAL INDEX

Absolute: existence shown by transcendental extension of being, 39; totality of reality is absolute, 40; notion of absolute, 40; nature of absolute reality, 41; hypothesis of several absolutes rejected, 84; absolute finite being a contradiction, 100, 138; is order of finite being absolute? 135, 138; solution to problem of the absolute, 141; the Infinite is an absolute being, 170; the necessarily existing being is the absolute, 249

Absolute Monism: see **Monism**

Absolute Pluralism: see **Pluralism**

Abstraction: idea of being is not abstract, 30; formal abstraction, 35; total abstraction, 36; formal and total are equivalent for being, 36

Accidents: embrace power of operation and second acts, 128; not proved from substance, 128; pantheism makes finite beings accidents, 189; God's thought not accidental, 199 sq.; creative act an accident, 223; finite beings need accidental activity as part of an order, 234. See also **Activity; Substance**

Act: used to define being, 26; realization of potency, 110; original meaning is dynamic, 110; secondary act a new perfection, 139; second act needed in finite beings, 234. See also **Act and Potency; Activity; Becoming; Potency**

Action: category of action belongs to special metaphysics, 252

Activity: used to define being, 26; activity and ontological goodness, 63; analysis of activity of finite beings, 118 sq.; activity of finite beings shows dynamism, 118 sq.; important type of

change, 118; psychological analysis of activity, 119 sq.; activity provides contact with non-self, 119; interpretation of metaphysical activity, 120; St. Thomas Aquinas on activity, 120; every finite being a principle of activity, 120; activity limited because of essence, 122; formal reason for activity is existence, 122; activity reveals new implications in finite, 125; subject of activity, 127; shows subject is relative, 129; illuminates nature of finite being, 130; activity of finite being shows dependence, 136; activity reveals basic dependence, 137; increases the whole finite order, 139 sq.; created finite beings must be active, 233 sqq.; the basic reason for activity of finite beings, 233; finite beings need accidental activity as part of an order, 234 sqq.; activity helps creature participate in perfection of Creator, 235. See also **Accidents; Contingent; Participation**

Act and Potency: relation to constitutive composition, 93, 112; properly refer to becoming, 93 sq.; Middle Ages broadened concepts, 94; Aristotle's theory of, 110; not comparable to existence and essence, 112 sq.; not had between subject and power of operation, 127. See also **Becoming; Change**

Ævum: see **Eviternity**

Affirmation: in derivation of God's attributes, 164

Agere sequitur esse: existence is formal reason for activity, 122

Agnosticism: and intelligibility of being, 57; absolute agnosticism rejected, 58; agnosticism regarding nature of God, 158; objections to knowledge of God, 161

238 sq.; immediate effect of, 239; problem distinct from problem of duration, 241 sq. See also **Conservation; Liberty, Divine**

Creationism: holds only the absolute is necessary, 222

Creative Cause: Aristotle did not know, 206

Deductive Method: used in ontology, 250

Definitions: which should be omitted from ontology, 251

Descartes, R.: recognized God as Mind, 200

Desirability: property of being, 61 sq.; metaphysical principle, 63; divine desirability a transcendental attribute, 191; divine love causes desirability of creatures, 220. See also **Good**

Desirable: finite being is desirable, 156

Desire: imperfect act of will, 62

Determinability: see **Perfectibility**

"Disexistentiation": of being impossible, 44 sq.

Disorder: suggested in nature, 134. See also **Order**

Dissimilarity, Principle of: constitutive composition, 92

Distinction: transcendental property of being, 49 sqq.; formula of the metaphysical principle, 50; metaphysical principle is basis for laws of logic, 50; transcendental attribute of God, 186

Distinction of Essence and Existence: historical note, 94 sq.

Diversity: of experience, 31; and being, 54; how seen in experience, 72 sqq.

Divine Names: see **God**

"Divine Subjectivism": the ideal knowledge, 206

Dualism: Manichean teaching refuted, 69

Duration: implied by existence, 176

Duties: God is not subject of, 203

Dynamic Composition: nature of, 126 sq.

Dynamic Order: do finite beings form this order? 132 sq.

Dynamism: moderate and absolute dynamism explains change, 108 sq.; shown in activity of finite being, 118 sqq.; holds order through activity, 131; dynamism proper to the corporeal world, 251. See also **Change; Activity**

Effect: pre-exists in cause, 192; effects of divine causality, see **Causality**

Efficient Cause: definition, 97

Elan Vital: doctrine of H. Bergson, 108; unfolding of inner dynamism, 117

Emanation: universe as necessary emanation of First Cause, 221. See also **Pantheism**

Emanationist Pantheism: see **Creationism**

Eminence: in derivation of God's attributes, 164

Empirical Method: used in ontology, 250

Empiricism: and definition of being, 25; Kantian Empiricism, 38; refuted by transcendental extension of being, 44; germ of absolute pluralism, 81; attacks intelligence, 82; hidden bent of, 144; refuted by use of transcendentalising method in ontology, 250; surpassed only by conceptual discursive thought, 255

End: of created persons, 221; of creation, 227

Enjoyment: perfect act of will, 61 sq.; God is Infinite Enjoyment, 201 sq.

Epistemology: connotations of immanence of God's knowledge, 205

Esse: used for component principle, 93; not potency for change, 111; determines subject or substance, 127

Essence: of being, 24; duality not implied in being, 28; positive element according to empiricist, 83; composition of, 86 sqq.; distinction between essence and existence, 94 sq.; not strictly a

INDEX OF PROPER NAMES